CATHERINE THE GREAT

CATHERINE

THE GREAT

BY KATHARINE SCHERMAN

Illustrated by PRANAS LAPÉ

RANDOM HOUSE · NEW YORK

Contents

1   Left-Handed Spirit 3

2   Elephants and Snow Slides 15

3   The Betrothal 33

4   The Marriage 50

5   The Revolution 69

6   Benevolent Despot 85

7   The Soldier-Monk 108

8   The Grandmother 130

9   End of the Dream 147

10   The Last Autocrat 166

Index 181

CATHERINE THE GREAT

1 Left-Handed Spirit

Russia in the eighteenth century was, to most Europeans, a dangerous, forbidding, barbaric country. Its nobles were richer than most European kings and queens. They lived in a state of extravagant idleness like sultans of The Arabian Nights, and they had hundreds of peasants whom they actually owned. The great mass of Russian people were no better than slaves. Travelers who were brave enough to go to Russia in those days found fantastic, decadent wealth contrasted with deepest poverty.

They also found beautiful, fertile land, millions of

square miles of it; and deep forests of tall virgin trees; and gorgeous cities built of many-colored stones and crowned with golden church spires; and unending hospitality, from the richest nobleman to the most miserable peasant. Surprisingly, they found gentleness among all the people, and much gaiety, and love for conversation and games and laughter.

They discovered too, from the highest to the lowest, the most abysmal ignorance and superstition.

Russia was the largest country in Europe, reaching from Poland to the border of China. Her vast boundaries were protected by armies of the bravest, strongest and most skillful soldiers in the world. And she was ruled by Czars who always wanted to make Russia just a little larger. Everybody in Europe was afraid of Russia—and with good reason. Its rulers were unpredictable, its people barbaric, its strength tremendous.

This is the story of a German princess to whom Russia was just such a fairy-tale, fearsome land as it was to everyone else. But she was to become its greatest ruler and to make herself the very spirit of this dangerous, wild, attractive country.

Catherine the Great was born Princess Sophie Friedricke Auguste on Sunday, May Day, 1729, in the grim, gray Prussian city of Stettin. She was the oldest child of Prince Christian August of Anhalt-Zerbst, a general in the service of King Frederick William I of Prussia. The good Prince had never shown brilliance or heroism, nor had anyone in his family. But he was strict and pious and very kind. For his unquestioning loyalty to his king, he had been given the governorship of the Prussian border city of Stettin.

It was a dull, puritanical town with heavy stone buildings and a perpetual cold, wet wind off the Baltic Sea. The Prince's royal employer was stingy so Christian August never had much money. But he was idealistic and austere, and he needed neither social gaiety nor wealth. He liked Stettin.

He had married, when he was thirty-seven, a girl of sixteen, Johanna, Princess of Holstein-Gottorp. She was as poor as her husband, but she was distantly related to the King of Sweden and the Empress of Russia. She had been brought up in the court of Brunswick, the showiest in all Europe. A lively and beautiful young lady, Johanna thought herself much too grand for prim, dowdy, church-going Stettin. Her children, she had determined even before she had any, should have more out of life than she.

But she was disappointed that her first child was a daughter. Wanting sons, Johanna took no interest in Sophie Friedricke Auguste, called Fike. The child was given to a succession of nurses. Stupid, nervous or indifferent, they found it impossible to curb the spirits of the too-lively Princess.

When Fike was an uncontrollable, unloved little wild animal of four, a new governess came. She was Babet Cardel, a French girl with a keen mind and a warm heart. Patient, cheerful and understanding, this young lady quickly won Fike's love. For ten years she was both mother and sister to the lonely princess. Fike learned young not to confide in anyone, but to Babet she told all her secrets.

Babet taught her the arts a young lady should know —drawing, embroidery, French and spelling. She also taught her to use her mind. When Fike did her lessons well, the governess rewarded her by reading aloud the plays of Molière, and explaining his sharp-witted philosophy to the receptive young student. Fike learned early that truth and reason were the only proper tools for a good mind.

Babet was sympathetic and entertaining; but she was also, under Johanna's orders, extremely strict with the young Princess. Politeness was important. "The word 'sir,' " Babet used to say, "never broke anybody's jawbone." Fike had to kiss the hems of the skirts of the ladies who visited her mother. Every day she was taken for a sedate walk, on which she was not allowed to play or run or to talk to anyone except Babet. If they met any of her mother's friends, Fike curtsied almost to the ground.

Still the lively little Princess found it pleasant to be outside her dark, ugly home, and see the sun and breathe the sea air. Inside the house she had to sit as still and prim as a doll. When she was seven, all her toys were taken away. Her mother told her that she was a grown-up girl, too old for playthings. But she invented toys out of handkerchiefs and scarfs, and played with them when, rarely, she was left alone for a few minutes.

She was seldom allowed to be by herself, even at night. Sometimes, long after bedtime, when the gloomy castle of the Governor was quiet and the city around it was dark and deserted, Fike heard strange sounds. Her room was right against the church tower, and through the thick wall she heard the organ playing eerily in the empty church. The servants, even Babet, had whispered fearfully that there were spirits in the church. But Fike knew better. There were no ghosts. If the organ was playing, then somebody was playing it—somebody who, like her, prized these rare moments of solitude. Wakeful and unafraid, the irrepressible Princess pulled the heavy bolster out from beneath her head, sat astride it in the middle of her big canopied bed, and rode an imaginary horse. Her black hair flew up and down as she galloped; her thin face was alive with excitement; and her blue eyes flashed in the dim light of the night candle. She dreamed grand dreams in the grim castle by the church tower.

Hasty footsteps approached her room. The horse turned quickly back into a pillow; and when Babet entered, the room was silent. Babet leaned over the bed and whispered "Fike," but saw only a peacefully sleeping child. The governess smiled to herself and went out. Wise Babet knew when it was better not to be too strict. Her little charge never had much fun. As the governess went down the hall, she heard the "horse" galloping again.

Every day Fike was given thorough lessons in religion, history and geography by her tutor, Pastor Wagner. She was an eager child and learned easily. But she always dreaded Pastor Wagner's coming, because he frightened her with his dreadful stories of the Last Judgment.

Still, even before the lessons began, she argued with him.

"What came before the Creation?" she would ask.

"Chaos," answered the pastor solemnly.

"And what came before chaos?" Fike persisted.

Herr Wagner turned red with anger and rose from

the table. "Mademoiselle Cardel," he called, "come and take this child. She is impudent. She needs the rod."

Fike turned with relief to Babet, who hurried her off, leaving Herr Wagner muttering behind them.

"My Fike, you must not tease the pastor," said Babet gently. "He is an old man, and he does his best."

"I wasn't teasing him," said Fike. "I only asked him a question, and he couldn't answer it."

"You are an *esprit gauche*, a left-handed spirit," said Babet affectionately. "You turn everything upside down and ask questions when you shouldn't."

But Fike's conscience was stronger than her impudence. Later, in the dim twilight of the winter afternoon, Babet found her hiding behind the curtain in her bedroom, weeping convulsively. Fike threw her arms around her governess. "Babet, what will happen to me? I will be eternally damned, and all those terrible things that Herr Wagner has promised will be done to me." Babet comforted her, and Herr Wagner never again spoke of the dreadful hereafter. Instead he would say drearily, "The joys of this world are not worth its pains." His pious and puritanical remarks sank like stones into the young mind, to stay there forever.

Special tutors were brought in for other subjects. Fike was obedient, but to Babet she made fun of these tutors. Her penmanship teacher, she said, spoke German like a Spanish cow. Her dancing teacher taught her to do steps on a small table like a marionette. Her music teacher was helpless with the tone-deaf child, who couldn't help disliking music. To make the les-

She was taught to do dance steps on a small table.

sons worse he always brought a baritone singer with him. Little Fike listened impatiently and said to herself, "He roars like an ox."

But she was repentant. When he had gone, she said sadly to Babet, "I long to hear and enjoy music, but in vain do I try. It is noise, and that is all." She added that the only tones she recognized were the barking of her nine dogs, each of whose voice she could distinguish instantly. In all her life, though she was to have many flatterers, no one ever praised her voice except one lute-maker, who told her she had a beautiful contralto. Fike, who hated flattery, retorted sharply that he only wanted to sell her a lute.

Fike was allowed to visit her mother for a few minutes twice a day. She ran down the long dark stone corridors as fast as she could to the wing of the mansion where Johanna lived. She ran, not only because she loved to see her mother, but also because she liked to run. In her mother's room the little Princess made a graceful curtsy and kissed the hand of the older Princess, who was not so much older.

Fike worshiped her pretty, romantic, vivacious young mother. But Johanna gave the child no love. Disappointed in her thin-faced and contrary daughter, Johanna alternately neglected her and scolded her unjustly. She lost no opportunity to tell Fike she was ugly. The young girl, not easily downcast, learned that she must find something in herself to take the place of beauty. She searched her soul seriously to find out what was there.

The two sons who followed Fike were the objects of their mother's passionate adoration, although one was constantly sick, the other crippled. But the frivolous Princess had no time even for them, and Fike took care of them. The learned little girl, who could memorize almost as fast as she could read, delighted in teaching her brothers everything she knew. Tender and loving, she was more of a mother to them than the vain Johanna.

In spite of her lack of affection, Johanna was extremely strict about Fike's upbringing. Her daughter must learn all the arts and graces suitable for a princess related to several of Europe's crowned heads. She must be fit to marry a prince—or even a king. Though Johanna did not expect much of her plain daughter, her ambitions were boundless.

Fike learned well. Along with history, geography, dancing and religion, she learned from her mother the importance of politics. And her determined young soul absorbed ambition from the determined older one.

But she never used unkindness as a tool for ambition. The austere, kindly father, though always in the background, was deeply a part of Fike's life. By his own example he taught her truth and compassion and justice. Sincerely religious, this upright man practiced as well as understood true Christianity. In the eighteenth century world of inequality and privilege and frivolity, the idealistic Prince taught his daughter the principles of democracy.

But not the sternest teachings of this stern German Lutheran household could curb Fike's lively, emotional and argumentative spirit. Her energy continually burst its strict bounds. She loved too much, she cried easily, she laughed even more easily, she questioned everything that seemed false to her—and no one could stop her.

When she was seven, she had an accident which would have broken the spirit of a less courageous child. While praying at the side of her bed one night, she coughed so hard that she fell and dislocated her spine. For three weeks she was in an agony of pain, and when she got out of bed she was in the form of a Z, right shoulder lifted and left side hollow. Her mother, desperately ashamed of her deformed daughter, would allow no one to see her except the doctor. The doctor said he could do nothing, that the only man in the town who had any skill with bones was the hangman.

"The hangman will not come in this house!" cried Johanna with all the horror of her snobbish soul. "Suppose someone should find out?"

But Fike got no better. At last the hangman was admitted secretly, late one night. He prescribed massages day and night, and made her a stiff, uncomfortable jacket which she was to wear all the time, even when she slept. In a year and a half she was straight again, but she had to wear the jacket for four years. The only lasting effect of this accident was that until the end of her life her posture was beautifully straight.

Though Fike's father felt quite at home in plain, gloomy Stettin, there was not enough room for the ambitious Johanna. Her husband was more than twice her age, and she considered him and his town unbearably stodgy. To get away from the wearisome piety of her home and make the most of her highborn connections, Johanna went on long visits to illustrious relatives. As soon as Fike could talk, she was taken along.

At the age of four Fike was presented to her father's

miserly employer, King Frederick William of Prussia. She made a deep, graceful curtsy, then went to kiss the hem of the King's coat. She could not reach it, and whispered to her mother, "Why does the King wear such a short coat? He is certainly rich enough to buy a longer one." The remark was truer than she realized.

The King asked what she had said. When he was told, he laughed sourly and said, "The maiden is saucy." But Fike smiled enchantingly at him, and the mean old King smiled back in sudden sympathy.

When she was eight, Fike was taken to the magnificent and formal court of Brunswick, where her mother had been brought up. For three or four months of every year until she was fourteen, the child took part in its ostentatious social whirl. Every day there were hunting parties and carriage drives, balls, operas, banquets and concerts. The little girl was allowed to stay up all night at masquerades. She could prattle as much as she liked, and she was spoiled by everyone except her mother. Johanna, as usual, either neglected her or scolded her. Johanna's friends at court chided her for the way she treated her daughter. "Madame," said one, "you do not know the child. I assure you, she has more mind and character than you give her credit for. I beg you to pay more attention to the maiden. Your daughter deserves it in every respect."

At eleven Fike still thought of herself as an ugly little girl. She did not take much care of her clothes, and coquetry was entirely foreign to her. Her portrait was painted, and Fike looked at it with dismay. "If it resembles me," she said sadly to her mother, "then you told me nothing false."

That year she went to a royal wedding in Brunswick. At the ball afterwards Prince Henry of Prussia, second son of the King, asked her continually for minuets and contredanses. Fike was enormously surprised when she heard one of the ladies whisper to another, "Watch the little Anhalt-Zerbst. She has Prince Henry at her feet."

For the first time in her life, after the ball was over, Fike studied herself in the mirror carefully and thoughtfully. She saw a slim girl, tall for her age, with straight, silky black hair, large blue eyes, a long chin, very white skin and a straight Grecian nose. She was not ugly, she thought—neither was she beautiful.

What she could not see was the gracious friendliness, the lively, irresistible charm, the tact and courtesy which had been trained in her, but which were also in her nature. Fike was no longer an incorrigible, left-handed spirit. She was turning into a real princess.

2 Elephants and Snow Slides

In 1739 Fike met her second cousin, Duke Karl Peter Ulrich of Holstein, called Peter, the eleven-year-old heir to the throne of Sweden with a strong claim to that of Russia. Her family had often teased her about this handsome cousin who might some day be her husband. She neither knew nor cared anything about marriage or love—she was only ten years old. But "husband" was a familiar word to an eighteenth-century princess from her earliest years, particularly if she had no dowry. Fike knew that her family was poor and that she had to marry well. So the clear-eyed little girl studied her cousin carefully.

The royal child looked too frail to carry the monstrous loads of massive Russia and warlike Sweden for which he was destined. He was pale and delicate and childlike, and whenever anyone crossed him he raved with ineffectual violence.

Peter was dominated and tormented by his chief tutor, a Prussian militarist named Bruemmer. This man subjected his feeble charge to a cruel and strict military regime. When the child did not do his lessons right, Bruemmer would punish him by depriving him of meals, beating him with a riding whip or making him kneel on dry peas with naked knees. As a result Peter, who was stupid to begin with, came to hate all study and could learn nothing. Bruemmer's only accomplishment was to make the little boy passionately fond of military drill. But Peter had no endurance. His idea of military maneuvers was to play with toy soldiers and drill the servants with a whip.

He was twitchy and nervous, could not sit still for five minutes and railed at everything in the least uncomfortable. Even at this young age his tutors had difficulty in keeping the self-indulgent boy from getting drunk at the table. In unconscious protest against his cruel teacher, he tortured animals and beat the servants with his weak fists. They were the only creatures to whom he could feel superior.

Fike, wise beyond her years, did not like what she saw. That man Bruemmer, she thought, was not even fit to train horses. She pitied the young Duke and kept her thoughts to herself. Peter did not hide his feelings toward Fike. He could not endure her. The Princess, outwardly well-behaved, was enviably free. She knew, within narrow limits, how to do exactly as she pleased without drawing attention to herself. Babet's healthy regime of love and look-the-other-way had made Fike a sane and happy child. But every step Peter made was regulated and counted. Bitterly he envied Fike her freedom and her naturalness.

Still they were only children. In spite of their differences, they were both lively, and soon they made friends. They played together with Peter's toy soldiers (though Fike had always hated dolls), and had games of tag and blindman's buff in the castle at Brunswick.

And they thought not at all about marriage.

Within four years Peter's life was suddenly changed —and with it the fate of the dowry-less Princess of Anhalt-Zerbst. Fike's mother, though she had looked on Peter with an interested eye, had not seriously considered him as a husband for her daughter. It was true he had a claim to two great thrones. But in the eighteenth century a kingdom went to him who was strongest. Peter had not the character to push his claims.

By 1742 Johanna changed her mind abruptly about Fike and Peter. That year Empress Elizabeth of Russia had sent for the young Duke, who was her nephew. The aging Empress was unmarried and longed for a son and heir. The throne of Russia was slippery—Elizabeth herself had taken it by revolution, imprisoning the rightful heir for life. Peter, heir to it by blood, could not become emperor unless Elizabeth wanted him to. The childless Empress had adopted the feeble, petulant child and immediately made him her heir. Peter formally gave up his claim to the throne of Sweden

He allowed himself to be made Grand Duke of Russia and surrendered completely to the smothering protection of the overbearing, hysterical and possessive Empress.

Now three worldly people put their heads together and cold-bloodedly concocted a marriage. Johanna, seeing a chance to ally her family with the most powerful throne in Europe, wrote loving letters to the Empress Elizabeth, whom she did not know at all. She reminded the Empress of her dead fiancé, who had been Johanna's brother, and sent her a pretty portrait of Fike.

Elizabeth was warmly responsive. She knew that Peter was not ready to marry. But she wanted an heir of the blood of her father, Peter the Great. The little Grand Duke *must* marry and *must* produce a child —and this must happen soon. He was frail and sickly, and any moment he might die.

The third member of the cynical trio, Frederick II of Prussia, had recently inherited the throne from his unpopular father. He wanted to increase the power of his small country by an alliance with Russia. He had two marriageable sisters but shrank from sending them into that dangerous, barbaric country. Well-brought-up European brides had been sent there before, and had sunk out of sight as if into quicksand. His eye lit on the young Princess of Anhalt-Zerbst, who had no dowry and whose family was loyal to him. They could hardly refuse their King's wishes. Frederick maneuvered busily behind the scenes in the Russian court and managed to cut out two more important princesses.

A perfect choice! An hysterical Empress, an ambi-

tious mother and a conscienceless politician decided
the fates of two children—a little girl full of love and
life, and a pathetic, stupid, neurotic little boy.

Fike's upbringing helped the scheme. Johanna had
exposed her to royalty from her earliest years; and
the idea of one day wearing a crown had been firmly
put into her head when she was seven. Innocent but
practical, the young Princess had decided that she
would marry the Grand Duke of Russia. She forced
herself to forget his petulant and unstable character
and remembered only that he was handsome, frail and
appealing.

On January 1, 1744, a fat letter with an impressive
seal was delivered to Fike's mother at dinner. Fike
recognized the seal and was suddenly excited. Silently,
eyes shining, she watched her mother read the letter.
When Johanna turned a page, Fike glimpsed the words,
"with the Princess, your eldest daughter," and immediately she knew the rest.

After dinner her mother and father locked themselves into their room. For three days the house was
full of suppressed excitement. People were called into
the closed room, and her mother and father continued
in ceaseless discussion. Fike was told nothing. On the
third day she could no longer control herself.

"This letter has set the house in an uproar, and
nobody consults me," she said to her mother. "But
I already know what is in it."

"What do you know?" asked Johanna.

"I know that we have been asked to go to Russia.
My powers of divination tell me."

Johanna was surprised, but she smiled. "Very good,

young lady," she said. "If you are so wise, perhaps you can tell me what is in the rest of this political letter of twelve pages."

"I will question my oracle," said Fike solemnly.

"You are a rogue, but you will learn nothing more about it."

Fike went to her room and came back with a slip of paper on which she had written, "The omens say, 'Peter III will be your husband.' "

Johanna was taken aback. On receipt of the letter from Russia she had suddenly become frightened. Her tardy mother love told her that this marriage was dangerous. Fike's father had been against it from the first. A republican at heart, he despised and feared the massive Russian autocracy. And as a pious Lutheran he did not want to trust his beloved fourteen-year-old daughter to the oriental pomp and luxury of the Russian court with its dangerous temptations.

But the web had been spun years before, and Fike was caught in it. She *would* go to Russia and she *would* marry her royal, witless cousin. She had set her mind on it with naïve determination. And Fike, then and later, was not a girl whose will could be crossed easily.

Johanna said tentatively, "Russia is a wild country. God knows what we will find there."

"God will take care of us, if such is His will," said Fike. "I have the courage to risk everything, and the voice of my heart tells me that all will go well." Then her adolescent courage suddenly forsook her, and she wept at the thought of leaving her home.

"We can always come back," she said.

Her father embraced her and said, "Go, and come

back if you want to. We have promised nothing." It was decided.

Babet had noticed Fike's feverish excitement in the past three days and saw the change now—the set, resolute face, the unusual paleness.

"What was in the letter?" she asked.

"I cannot tell you." For the first time Fike turned away from her governess.

"If you love me, you must tell me," said Babet. Fike's determined silence worried her.

"Do you think it would be right for me to tell something which has been forbidden?" Fike asked, turning to Babet. Then suddenly she was in tears. They put their arms around each other, and Babet wept too.

"I'm only going to Berlin," Fike insisted over and over, sobbing.

The family left almost immediately—Fike, her mother and father. But Babet was left behind. They traveled incognito and without servants. Johanna did not want anyone to know where they were bound, in case they should fail and have to come home again.

They stopped in Berlin for a day. There Frederick II insisted on entertaining them. Johanna, wanting secrecy and still ashamed of her plain daughter, tried to prevent it. She said Fike had no proper clothes. But the King sent Fike a ball dress belonging to one of his sisters and commanded that she appear for dinner. Fike, in an agony of shyness and embarrassment, was seated next to the King. As a little girl she had prattled unthinkingly in the presence of the most august persons. Now she was going to be married, and she was supposed to act like a grown-up court lady. But she still felt like a little girl. Frederick, the good politician, put her at ease with grace and charm. He talked to her courteously all evening. By the end of the dinner Fike was completely captivated. Frederick handed her a sweet and told her to give it to a handsome gentleman who had come up behind her chair.

"Accept this gift from the hand of the Loves and Graces," said Frederick with ostentatious gallantry. Fike blushed violently and could think of nothing to say.

But Frederick had achieved his aim. He did not underestimate Fike's firm and ambitious character, and he guessed that she would one day be a power. He had won the little girl's heart and had made himself an important future ally at the changeable court of the Empress Elizabeth.

The next morning Fike, her father and mother drove away from Berlin in a closed carriage. At the gates of the city Fike had to say good-bye to her father. The invitation from Russia had specifically excluded the Prince of Anhalt-Zerbst. The schemers were afraid that this stern and upright man would prevent the marriage. He put into Fike's hand a long list of instructions telling her to be a good, pious and quiet girl in the midst of temptations. Then he embraced her and left. Fike, in tears again, realized with sudden force that with her father her childhood had departed. But his austere kindliness, his intellectual idealism and his stern sense of justice had entered into Fike's spirit and would sustain her all her life long.

As they drove east, the travel became increasingly uncomfortable. But Fike's irrepressible good humor had returned. She enjoyed everything. Most exciting was the huge comet that appeared over Courland, north of Poland. Its gleaming golden tail seemed almost to touch the earth.

As Fike's spirits lifted with the new sights, Johanna's declined. Wishing their journey to be secret, they had to sleep at the post stations where the horses were changed. Johanna was depressed by the humbleness of their travel and wrote complaining letters to her husband:

"As the rooms in the stations are not heated we are obliged to go into the common room, which is not unlike a pigsty: the master and mistress, the house dog, the cook and the children—children everywhere, in cradles, in beds, on the stove, on mattresses—everything is rolled together in disorder like weeds and roots. There is nothing else to be done: I order a bench to be brought in and lie down in the middle of the room. My daughter is so healthy and cheerful that I must wonder at it. Really I would need an iron constitution to keep up my resistance. Fike is more fortunate. Her youth supports her health, and like the young soldiers who scorn danger because they do not know about it, she delights in every difficulty."

They entered Russia at Riga, on the northeastern border. Leo Narishkin, Chief Master of the Hunt, a gay and handsome young man, met them as the big guns of the town saluted. He presented them with long sable capes lined with gold brocade and a beautiful fur carriage rug, presents from Empress Elizabeth. Fike touched the rich fur with awe. "I have never had fur before," she said. A reception was held for them. Suddenly everything had changed, and they felt like princesses again.

Immediately Narishkin took them on to St. Peters-

The sleighs sped over the bright snow to St. Petersburg.

burg. Russia was a new, fairy-tale world. Fike's eyes shone continually, and she laughed at everything. The sleighs, lined with fur rugs, looked like large cradles. Each held but one person, lying down. Fike laughed as she tried awkwardly to get into one.

Her sturdy peasant driver wore a garment that looked like a sheepskin nightgown reaching from his neck to his heels, fur mittens, a huge fur cap, fur shoes and rags wrapped around his legs instead of stockings. He sang all the time as he drove, brandishing his big whip over the strong, furry little horse.

They sped over the glistening snow to St. Petersburg. No bush or tree marked the road, and everything was covered with deep snow. But the horses knew their way unerringly and never stopped galloping. Sometimes in the distance Fike heard a faint tinkling—the bells of another sleigh far ahead in the whiteness. An infinite multitude of little shining golden darts no bigger than hairs—sun-touched frost particles—flew in all directions through the cold air. Fike saw two suns, one real one, the other reflected palely in the frozen moisture of the air.

In St. Petersburg they were greeted again with the thunder of cannon and immediately were taken to the palace. Empress Elizabeth was living in Moscow, her winter residence; but many members of her court had stayed behind to greet the German Princesses. Dressed magnificently, the ladies and gentlemen were drawn up on the wide marble staircase to present themselves when Fike and her mother entered. Fike, at the height of joyous good spirits, forgot to be awed by this pompous display.

After the formal introduction she sat down to a very grand dinner with the nobles and aristocracy of the city. Fike's family, not being wealthy, had never known extravagant meals. Indeed she did not know what she was eating, and Narishkin told her—sterlet, a small, delicate sturgeon, from the Volga, veal from Archangel, pheasants from Bohemia, beef from the Ukraine, champagne from France, beer from England and grapes from Astrakhan.

After dinner Narishkin took them into the courtyard, where they were treated to a display of fourteen tame elephants which had been presented to the Empress by the Shah of Persia. Then they went for a drive. St. Petersburg was only forty years old. Peter the Great had built it in 1703, all at once, needing a capi-

tal for the new northern empire he had won from
Sweden. He had used slave labor, and the slaves were
careless. The city was not well built; it was already
crumbling. But it was beautiful, with wide paved
streets and Italian-style houses painted pink, blue or
yellow, with many tall windows and dainty balconies.
Through it ran the river Neva, now solid with ice and
looking like a broad avenue. The river was flanked on
one side by the royal palace and the stately government buildings; on the other by the immense, frightening pile of the fortress.

Fike looked at the grim fortress and shuddered. St.
Petersburg was a symbol of the new, powerful and
dangerous Russia. She knew, as all Europe did, what
it had cost to build this fabulous southern city in the
midst of a frozen northern marsh. She wondered privately how many slave lives had been lost in the building of that great ugly citadel.

But the little seed of fear was quickly forgotten
when Narishkin stopped the carriage to let her watch
a trotting race on the frozen river Neva. Each tiny,
elegant sleigh was driven by its owner, a beautifully
dressed nobleman. Beside every sleigh was a mounted
servant in the fur-trimmed uniform of a hussar.
Though the servants galloped full speed they could not
keep up with the twinkling legs of the small, deep-
chested trotting ponies, whose long tails floated out
behind them while their silky manes almost swept the
ground.

Fike was beside herself with delight when she saw
her first ice slide. It was a scaffolding sixty feet high,
with stairs on one side, and on the other a narrow runway covered with ice, so steep it was almost vertical,

down which sped little sleds. Fike heard shrieks and laughter from the throngs around the slide. She wanted to try it. She climbed the steep stairs, and at the top was told to seat herself in the lap of the guide in the little sled. Faster than light they sped down the glassy runway. Fike did not even have time to catch her breath for a scream. She slid down again and again, and did not want to leave when Narishkin told her it was time for supper.

After supper the company played cards. Fike had never had any money of her own and knew nothing about gambling. She watched fascinated as the noble ladies and gentlemen applied themselves grimly to their favorite pursuit. They did not seem to enjoy it much, and hardly a word was spoken in the vast salon. Don't they know how to talk, wondered Fike. Or perhaps they had nothing to talk about.

The next morning two young ladies of the court came to Fike's room and started playing with her long black hair.

"There is a fashionable new hairdo," they said. "Let us try it on you." They fussed over her for more than an hour with pins, ribbons and curling irons. When they were through, Fike looked at herself in the mirror and burst out laughing. She looked like a doll. In the middle of each cheek was a stiff little curl fastened to her dimple with glue. A broad ribbon was tied around her head just above the forehead; its ends hung down to her neck and were stuck full of flowers. More flowers hung over her cheeks on loops of ribbon. In the back was a huge, intricate chignon; and from it flowed more ribbons, down to her waist. Fike thought she had never seen anything so absurd as the yards of ribbon and the stiff little curls. Hair styles, she learned, changed constantly at court, according to the whim of the Empress. Fike could not know that this one was already out of favor with Elizabeth.

After two days Fike had to give up the delights of elephants, ice slides and new hairdos. They must get to Moscow in time for Peter's birthday. A train of thirty big sleighs set out from St. Petersburg, each one drawn by ten horses. In this far northern country there were only a few hours of daylight in winter, so huge bonfires burned to light their way along the snowy highway. All around them were miles of flat snow, shifting and dangerous under the relentless north wind. There were few villages, and they were almost hidden under the snow. Sometimes the train passed the ghost of a village, where the ragged shells of burned huts stood silent and menacing in the twilight. Near it were the crumbling remains of a splendid country palace. Fike learned that in the extreme heat of summer entire villages often burned down. The homeless peasants had to walk from town to town begging, in order to gain enough to rebuild. Even the castles, built of soft limestone, could not withstand the excessive heat of summer and the bitter cold of winter. This remote country began to seem desolate and threatening.

But Fike's curiosity easily overcame her faint forebodings. They often stopped at villages to change horses and rest for a while at the post station. There they were given hot coffee and fish soup. And Fike, irrepressibly curious, wandered along the village street to peer into the cottages.

The village invariably consisted of a single long

street, lined with identical huts. They were built of logs with the bark stripped off, fastened at the end with wooden pegs. Their roofs, steeply peaked and thatched with straw, overhung the walls so the snow could slip off easily. Fike tried to look through the tiny square windows. Through dense smoke she could sometimes see people eating from wooden plates with wooden spoons. The most delicious odors came out of the houses—pickles, smoked fish and meat, cabbage soup and a peppery, gingery smell which she was told afterwards was *izbiten*. This was an ancient drink which the Russian peasants enjoyed instead of expensive tea. It was made of pot herbs, ginger, pepper and honey, all boiled together. Fike longed to buy some from the old men who sold it on the streets, dealing it out in tumblers. But it was only a common person's drink, she was told.

Sometimes she was hospitably invited inside a hut, and she had to bend double in order to get through the low door. She could not speak Russian, but she smiled and the family smiled, and then they all laughed at their efforts to understand one another.

Most of the huts had only one room, into which were crowded the whole family and a good deal of the livestock. A huge brick stove was the main article of furniture; there were mats and sheepskins on top of it, for here the family slept in the winter. The stoves had no chimneys so the huts were filled with smoke, which gradually found its way out of the little windows or the low door. Through the smoky darkness Fike could see a table made of rough-hewn fir planks evidently cut out with a hatchet, a chest for clothes and a wooden trough carved out of a tree, for washing clothes. These were ranged along one side of the room. Directly opposite the door was a row of wooden ikons —pictures of saints—crudely painted and dark with age and smoke. People always bowed to the ikons as they entered and crossed themselves several times before they greeted the household. The worship of these idols offended Fike's Lutheran spirit.

In every village there was at least one public house where vodka was sold very cheaply. The arms of Russia, the imperial eagle, were over the door of every public house, and there were fir boughs at the windows. From within came a perpetual sound of drunken revelry. Every now and then a burly peasant would be thrown out the door, yelling rich Russian obscenities. These saloons were open all day and all night. They were owned by the government, which had a monopoly on the sale of liquor. The Russian people loved to drink, and the government encouraged them in order to make millions of rubles selling vodka.

All in all, thought Fike, these sturdy, red-cheeked, handsome peasants, though barbaric, seemed to live well. They did not look like the downtrodden slaves her father had led her to expect. She heard singing and laughter as the young people played on their rough little ice slides. The children tumbled happily all over the snow, dressed lightly but not seeming to notice the cold. Their mothers, in fur boots and gay plaid shawls, were broad-cheeked and fat and friendly.

She did not yet know that, having so little, the Russian peasant always shared what he had, thinking that another might be even poorer than he. And, having no future, no security and no hope of ever owning any worldly goods, he took refuge in laughter, song, childish games and drunkenness. She did not know of the hopeless, abysmal ignorance; the impenetrable dark superstition which passed for religion; the total ownership of serf by lord, so that a serf could never call a wooden spoon or a single ruble his own, and a man could be taken from his wife without a word spoken.

To fourteen-year-old Fike, brought up in gentleness, entirely ignorant of the world outside Molière and the polite courts of Europe, the Russian peasants seemed like gay characters in an opera. She had learned from her father the principles of equality, justice and freedom for everyone. But in her young mind they were still only abstract theories.

At the end of three days the travelers approached Moscow. In the distance, across the long waste of snow, they saw golden spires, like a vision of a fairy-tale city. Coming closer they topped a small hill; and suddenly the entire great city was spread out before them, stretched in the form of a crescent, twenty-six miles around. Innumerable towers, spires and domes glittered in the light of the setting sun. White, red and green buildings shone brightly as if newly painted. The Moscow River wound gracefully around many-colored palaces; and even the wooden hovels clustered around the stately houses seemed touched with magic in the golden, snowy twilight.

Fike caught her breath. The city was tremendous and beautiful and strange. But it was to be her home. Pride and awe filled her. Solemnly the little girl made three silent resolutions:

"One: I will please Peter.

"Two: I will please Elizabeth.

"Three: I will please the nation."

She had been in her new country for a whole week. She loved it, and she felt strong and sure as she entered Moscow.

3 The Betrothal

Johanna and her party halted just within the city limits to change their clothes. There they were given elaborate state sleighs, each one drawn by sixteen horses. At eight o'clock in the evening they started for the palace.

Someone handed Johanna a court journal containing character descriptions of all the most important people at the court. She read this assiduously as the train crossed Moscow. Already she was planning how best to stay in favor with the Empress. Fike did not listen to the bits of gossip her mother handed out from time to time. She was concerned only with the dark, snowy city. She saw a watchman standing by a fire on a street corner, banging the half hour on a big iron triangle. She saw palaces whose windows blazed with the light of hundreds of candles. The large grounds around each palace contained orchards, gardens, stables, outhouses, innumerable huts. The palaces were of every conceivable size and style, as though each lord had built according to his fancy. It looked as though several hundred noblemen's castles had come to live together, each bringing its attendant village—and that was exactly what it was. In winter each nobleman moved to Moscow with his entire retinue—musicians, actors, shoemakers, mechanics, chimney sweeps, watchmakers, painters—often numbering several hundred.

There were more churches than Fike had ever seen in her life. Each one had a tall, gilded spire with a cross on top and a cluster of shining, onion-shaped domes of copper or tin.

Moscow's great bell, famous all over Europe, was pointed out to her. "We Russians," explained Narishkin, "have a strange ambition to make big things. The truth is that the sound of this bell would deafen everyone. But it cannot ring." He told her the history of the bell. Ten years before Empress Anna had ordered it to be made for one of the church towers of the Kremlin. It weighed two hundred tons; its metal was two feet thick, and its clapper weighed a ton. When it was finished, the workmen could not move it; and there it stayed, silent on the ground.

"But we are delighted with it," concluded Narishkin with a laugh.

(Later, in 1812, when Napoleon came to Moscow

with his army and set the city on fire, the bell got red hot. Someone poured water on it, and it cracked wide open. It is still there.)

It took the royal guests an hour and a half to cross this strange city, part squalid village, part elegant capital. There seemed to be no end to it. And in fact it had the largest area of any city in Europe, although its population was relatively small.

They were met at the palace by the Prince of Hessen-Homburg, the head of the court, who bowed low, took Johanna's hand and led them to their apartments. As they were taking off their caps and furs, Peter came in. He embraced them both and said gracefully, "The last half hour of waiting has been so unbearable that I would have liked to harness myself to your sleigh to hasten your coming."

The Grand Duke had acquired some court polish since Fike had seen him last, four years before. But he still appeared childlike and sickly, and he was a good two inches shorter than she although he was more than a year older. They exchanged courtly compliments until word came from the Empress ordering them to her apartments. The Prince of Hessen-Homburg took Fike's hand; Peter took Johanna's, and they passed through a succession of vast salons. The whole court was lined up to be introduced, and everyone stared at the visitors curiously from head to foot. Fike felt that she was turning red from the intense scrutiny.

But the Russians liked what they saw: a tall, well-made girl who held herself with graceful dignity. She was not yet beautiful, but she had a pleasant and friendly expression. She wore a close-fitting dress without hoop skirts, of rose-colored moire trimmed with silver. Compared to the gaudy finery of the Russian ladies her dress was simple. But her youth and happiness were so apparent that she needed no ornament.

When they came into the presence of the Empress, the two German Princesses curtsied to the ground, bowing their heads. Elizabeth came forward to raise them, and Fike looked with awe at this queenly person. The Empress was tall and very stout. But she moved with freedom and grace. Her head was beautiful, and she gave the impression at once of warmth and great majesty. She wore a dress of shining silver taffeta trimmed with gold lace, its skirt stiffened with an enormous hoop skirt. Her black hair was elaborately dressed and glittered with diamonds, and a black ostrich feather stood upright on one side of it. The innocent Fike, who had been told nothing of the character of this frivolous and dissolute Empress, liked her immediately.

Elizabeth greeted Johanna first. They exchanged politenesses in French. Then Fike was introduced and more French phrases were spoken. For half an hour the formalities continued. Although there were chairs, Elizabeth did not sit down so everyone had to stand. Finally the guests were excused and went to have supper. Elizabeth did not eat with them but covertly watched Fike and Peter from a door.

The next day, Peter's birthday, was one of show and pomp. Wearing a brown taffeta dress embroidered with silver, her head, neck and bodice entirely covered with jewels, Elizabeth presented the Order of St. Catherine to Johanna and Fike. The rest of the day the court trailed Elizabeth from church to church for religious ceremonies.

The first days were extremely formal. Fike and her mother paid and received visits, waited on Elizabeth in the late afternoons and played cards sedately with Peter in the evenings until ten o'clock. Fike was friendly and warm-hearted, but her natural reserve kept her out of the court intrigues in which Johanna immediately involved herself. Fike watched and learned and wondered, even as she pleased everyone with her spirited good humor. Soon she started to learn Russian and decided to take instructions in the Greek Orthodox religion. She wanted to become as Russian as possible.

Thoughtful and self-probing, Fike's decision to embrace a religion which seemed to her almost pagan cost her a terrible effort. The spirit of her pious Lutheran father rose within her in revolt, and Pastor Wagner's hellfire appeared to her in agonizing dreams. The crisis came the day Elizabeth left on one of her innumerable visits to a monastery for fasting and prayer. She came to say good-bye to Fike, wearing a long-sleeved dress of black velvet decorated with all the Russian orders for women—the Order of St. Andrew as a scarf, the Order of St. Alexander around her neck and the Order of St. Catherine at her left side. The magnificent Empress did not look like one who was about to spend days in religious contemplation and self-denial.

Fike looked at her in wonder and was suddenly hit with sharp disgust. Observant and clear-eyed, she had come to know much about the habits of this barbaric

Queen. Elizabeth loved both drink and food to excess. She had innumerable favorites, whom she changed frequently and who themselves could change the entire personnel of the court within a few days. A passionate gambler, she would win or lose forty or fifty thousand rubles at her table in an evening. She was usually the last one to leave the card table, seldom earlier than two o'clock. She would then have supper and would never go to bed before sunrise. She had 10,000 dresses and 5,000 pairs of shoes.

The sharp contrast between Elizabeth's fanatical devotion to religion and her self-indulgent and frivolous daily life pierced the pious German Princess like a sword. She saw now that these traits, extreme in Elizabeth, were true also of all the Russian ladies she had met. Both traits were violently alien to Fike. There was nothing either mystical or self-indulgent in her sane, orderly German character. She felt an intense personal revolt at these extremes.

Fike had amazing self-discipline for such a young girl. She had spent long nights studying the Russian language and religion, barefoot, to keep awake. She had shown no one a hint of her hard work and her unceasing fight with her conscience. But the silent struggle had been a strain. And this interior revulsion was suddenly too much for her fourteen-year-old strength. That night she fell ill and for the next twenty-seven days was alternately delirious or unconscious.

The doctors wanted to bleed her immediately. But Johanna was terrified at the thought and forbade it. A messenger was sent to Elizabeth, who came back from the monastery at once. Still in her black velvet dress, she swept into Fike's room, imperiously ordered Johanna out of it, and held the unconscious child in her arms while the doctor bled her.

Fike was bled sixteen times during her illness. After each bleeding she became briefly conscious. She noticed Elizabeth hovering over her and her mother in a far corner of the room, looking unhappy.

Once she heard Johanna say, "We must call a Lutheran pastor. The child is near death."

Fike rallied her failing strength and spoke: "No, call Simon Todorsky rather. I would like to speak with him." Simon Todorsky was her instructor in the Greek religion. Fike had won her fight with her conscience.

Unknowingly she had also made a triumph of diplomacy. Elizabeth was now openly devoted to her and showered her with expensive gifts as she slowly got well. Peter came to see her every day and appeared to like her. She was accepted by everyone as the perfect bride for the Grand Duke.

Johanna wrote triumphantly to her husband: "Our daughter makes a very good impression here. The thing is done!"

Fike's first appearance after her illness was on her fifteenth birthday. Elizabeth looked at her critically and told her that she was too pale; she must wear rouge. Fike had never used paint. But all the ladies of the court colored their lips, cheeks and eyes and powdered or dyed their hair. They changed their costumes several times a day and seemed to have no occupation other than adorning themselves or playing cards. In the depth of her mind Fike was critical, but she set out to do as they did. She was determined to become a perfect Russian.

On this day also Elizabeth gave Fike the first money she had ever owned—for gambling. Fike did not know how to gamble, nor did she wish to. But she loved to be generous. The money Elizabeth gave her, which was the first installment of a large allowance, went almost entirely in gifts. Brought up in a parsimonious home Fike expanded with the unaccustomed luxury. Delightedly she scattered expensive presents right and left until even the spendthrift Elizabeth was shocked.

After the crisis with her conscience had been successfully passed, the glittering pomp of Elizabeth's court was heady wine to the young Princess. But she had work to do also. She took up her Russian lessons again and pleased Elizabeth by writing her little letters in Russian. Her confession for her religious conversion was written for her in Russian by Simon Todorsky. It was fifty pages long, and she memorized it. She practiced speaking it for hours every day and had long discussions with her teachers as to which of the Russian dialects she should use.

On June 28, 1744, five months after she had entered Russia, Fike was confirmed in the Greek Orthodox Church. She stood at the altar of the enormous domed cathedral, which gleamed with gold and many-colored stone mosaics, and recited her long confession in a clear voice with a faultless accent. She wore a dress of heavy crimson silk, and around her head was a white ribbon. She had no ornament except a pair of diamond earrings that Elizabeth had given her. Her shining black hair was unpowdered, and her cheeks were untouched by rouge. Her customary paleness was enhanced by three days of fasting before the cere-

Fike was confirmed in the Greek Orthodox Church.

mony; and her skin, against the black hair and the brilliant dress, looked almost transparent.

The clear young voice and the ethereal and noble appearance of the Princess moved many of the audience to tears. Elizabeth covered her face with her hands, and the romantic Johanna wept openly. Fike herself did not weep. Her face had no expression except one of calm dignity as Sophie Friedricke Auguste became Catherine Alexeievna. She had deliberately turned her back on the past, and willingly accepted a new life and a new name.

(Elizabeth had superstitiously insisted on the change of name, because Sophie was a name of a sister of Peter the Great, who had plotted against him. Catherine Alexeievna was the name of Elizabeth's mother, Peter's wife, who had reigned after his death as Catherine I.)

The day after Fike became Catherine, her betrothal to Peter took place. Together the children stood before the bishop in the cathedral and formally exchanged rings—tiny marvels given them by Elizabeth, which cost 14,000 rubles each. If Catherine felt dismay as she looked at the puny and ill-tempered child who was to be her husband, she took care not to show it.

Catherine was now "Her Imperial Highness, the Grand Duchess," and next to the Empress she was the most important lady at court. As she, with Peter and her mother, entered Elizabeth's presence after the ceremony, Johanna dropped back, as she was supposed to, and gave precedence to her daughter. Catherine blushed deeply. She was still in awe of her pretty mother and felt like an ugly little girl whenever Johanna was near. After that she carefully avoided any situation which might force her to pass in front of her mother.

After the betrothal a ball took place at the foot of the throne. Only the highest ladies and gentlemen danced in this tiny space; the others used the rest of the room. Catherine felt nearly smothered with the heat and the crowd, and was relieved when at last the long and formal day was over.

Now began two months of constant celebration. Elizabeth dragged her court all over the country as she moved capriciously from one summer palace to another. At first Catherine found this traveling pointless and dull. Often members of the court had to wait many days while Elizabeth went hunting along the way. While they waited, there was nothing to do except play cards, which she hated. Even more stupid, thought the Grand Duchess, were the endless, extravagant and disorganized entertainments put on for the royal visitors in every town.

But Catherine was only fifteen years old. Her early childhood, in a pious, parsimonious and sickly home, had not been much fun. The Russian court was a continuous festival. Catherine, gay and good-humored by nature, could not stay critical for long. She and Peter laid down mattresses in their carriage and made it into a playhouse, where they bounced and screamed the whole day with their teen-aged ladies- and gentlemen-in-waiting. At the palaces Catherine rose early in the morning and danced with her maids until breakfast. She took ballet lessons from the court dancing master just so that she could have an excuse to dance. She had lessons on the piano from the leader of Elizabeth's Italian orchestra—that is, he played while she danced around the room. Almost every night there was a ball, and she danced again.

One of Elizabeth's favorite forms of entertainment was a masquerade in which the men dressed as women and the women as men. The Empress loved to dress as a man, and in spite of her stoutness she looked remarkably handsome. But her court hated these balls. The men, ugly and awkward in their gowns, did not know how to handle the gigantic hoop skirts and were constantly knocking people over with them. The women were miserable in their unbecoming costumes, and the whole company was in a bad humor. Only the merry little German Grand Duchess thought these affairs funny. Once her tall partner tripped over his hoop skirt and knocked over both Catherine and a woman behind him. All three found themselves on the floor hopelessly entangled in the courtier's voluminous skirts. Each time one tried to get up, another would fall again. Catherine was helpless with laughter. Finally they all had to be lifted up at once and carried off the floor to be untangled.

Elizabeth had given Catherine eight Russian maids-in-waiting, all young. Alternately Catherine romped with them and ordered them about imperiously. She handed out duties to each maid: one had the key to her jewels, another her linen, another her laces, another her dresses, another her ribbons, another her paint, pins and patches. She ordered them all to do their hair the way she did hers, cut short in the front and curled into a frizzled bang. Some wept and refused, saying they would look like "birds with a topknot." But the dictatorial young Duchess insisted. She took them out on a midnight walk in the garden, for which they were all soundly scolded the next day. She took the lid off the piano and made a slide out of it from the sofa to the floor. Every evening after supper she and her maids slid down the piano lid, played blindman's buff and raced all over the room. Catherine imitated the voices and walks of birds and animals until her maids were weak with laughter.

She was feverishly gay, as though she were trying to crowd a whole life of fun into the few months before her marriage.

One day Catherine was taken to task for her frivolity by an intellectual German friend. He gave her a reproachful sermon which reminded her of Herr Wagner: "How comes it that your character, which was strong and competent, permits itself to grow effeminate at this court which is ruled by luxury and pleasure? Your gifts were granted you in order that you might accomplish great things, and you condescend to this childishness! I should like to wager that you have not had a book in your hands since you came to Russia."

Catherine was immediately ashamed and earnestly promised that she would read and become more serious-minded. He gave her *Plutarch's Lives*, the *Life of Cicero* and the *Causes of the Greatness and Decline of the Roman Republic*. Catherine looked with dismay at these heavy volumes and picked up the last one. She read a sentence and yawned. She read another sentence and fell into a dream.

"That must be a very good book," she thought, "but I will read it some other time." She threw it down and went back to her dressing table.

But her German friend continued to try to make her strengthen her character and told her she must look into her soul. Catherine, feeling guilty again, struggled with herself. Then she thought and wrote for many days. She produced a long essay which she called "Attempt at a portrayal of the character of a fifteen-year-old philosopher." In spite of its pompous title this essay was remarkably keen and shed light into the most secret corners of her mind. Young as she was, Catherine knew how to probe into her own flaws.

In writing this self-study she discovered what was the chief cause of her wild and childish behavior—she was trying to cover a growing uneasiness.

During her illness Peter had come to see her every day and had appeared to like her. He chattered to her for hours about his playthings and his toy soldiers. Catherine listened to him agreeably, but she often yawned without knowing why. Now that they were betrothed, Catherine saw a great deal of him. She saw how his tutors neglected him or else treated him harshly and clumsily. His desires and passions could not be controlled; he drank too much and often fell into childish rages in which he beat his servants. He trained his lackeys and valets in military drill and played endlessly with toy soldiers. Catherine was the only person who did not try to improve him. She simply listened to him in a friendly and sympathetic manner, and so she was the only one he talked to.

But it did not matter much to him whether he came to her or not—actually he preferred to play by himself with his dolls. And never at any time did he show her the tenderness of a lover.

Catherine did not let anyone know or guess that she thought herself unloved. She had too much pride and self-respect. But she cried often when she was alone, and took refuge in feverish gaiety when she was in company.

They had only been betrothed a few weeks when Peter got smallpox. He was ill for six weeks. When Catherine saw him again, her blood congealed in horror. The pale, childish good looks had vanished. Peter had become a monster, his face swollen and disfigured by terrible scars.

As the wedding day approached, Peter showed less and less desire to be with her. Catherine grew sadder and more frightened. She knew by now that this would be a hopelessly bad marriage. But she had no one to turn to. She did not dare confide in her maids; for she knew that the Russian court was full of spies. She could not talk to her mother, who was unsympathetic, jealous and deeply involved in court intrigues. And she had to appear normal, friendly and happy before Elizabeth and the court. It was a heavy burden for a fifteen-year-old girl. She spoke to herself sternly and hardened her heart:

"If you love this man you will be the most unhappy creature on God's earth; he scarcely takes any notice of you. He hardly talks of anything but dolls. You are too proud to complain about it. So take care, please, regarding any tenderness towards this gentleman. Think of yourself, Madame."

On her wedding day Catherine was up at six o'clock, and at eight she went to Elizabeth's room, where the palace ladies were waiting to dress her. Her dress was of silver glacé, with silver embroidery at all the seams. It was as heavy and stiff as a suit of armor. The Empress herself placed on Catherine's head the cumbersome, jewel-encrusted ducal crown, which she had to wear all day. At ten o'clock they started for the cathedral, but it was one o'clock before the long, slow, grand procession was finished. The dreary, formal ceremony in the cathedral lasted three hours, during which Catherine stood unmoving, her face pale with strain and fatigue. First the bishop intoned a long, weighty sermon. Then two golden wedding crowns were held over the heads of Peter and Catherine while the marriage was consecrated.

During one part of the ceremony a lady came up behind Peter and whispered something in his ear.

"Get you gone!" Peter hissed, turning his head. "What nonsense!"

The lady had told him, he whispered to Catherine, not to turn his head while he stood before the priest. Whichever one did this first must be the first to die. A cold shiver ran over Catherine. Peter had turned his head first.

After the wedding there was a banquet. By this time Catherine was weary from standing all day in her stiff wedding gown, and she had a fearful headache from the weight of the crown. She begged to be allowed to take it off for a few minutes, but it was not permitted. The ladies thought it might be an evil omen.

"The plague take this omen-ridden country," thought Catherine miserably. She was near fainting, and finally one of the ladies got Elizabeth's reluctant permission to remove the crown during dinner. She had to put it on again for the ball, at which only slow, formal polonaises were danced. Catherine moved through this like a marionette, her lips forming stiff smiles, her feet moving automatically.

Those who saw her thought, for the first time, that she was beautiful. She looked fine-drawn and delicately pale under the enormous medieval crown; and her figure was touchingly girlish in the stiff, elaborate gown. But the last weeks of fear, unhappiness and self-discipline had put lines of firmness into her young face and given it beauty and character beyond her years.

She looked at her silly, pathetic and unbalanced husband and thought, not for the first time, "I will do my best."

4 The Marriage

After the wedding there were ten days of festivities. The air was full of the roar of cannons and the sound of bells. In the public square before the palace, were huge pyramids of food topped with whole roasted bullocks, their horns painted gold. Hogsheads of wine were laid in the streets and spouted continuously like fountains. There were fireworks every night. And in the palace there was a succession of formal balls and masquerades.

But Catherine could no longer enjoy the extravagant frivolity. From the day of the marriage her life had changed. At the balls she found herself paired with men aged sixty to ninety, lame, gouty and decrepit. Elizabeth did not want her nephew's wife to know any young people. The Grand Duchess, who had so loved to dance, moved through the steps of the stiff quadrilles in white-faced misery, tears in her eyes.

She could not please Elizabeth now. She was always being accused of something, no matter what she did. If she visited Peter often, it was said that she wanted to intrigue with those around him. If she saw him less, she was scolded for not being nice to him. If she looked sad, they said, "She is satisfied with nothing." If she was merry, they suspected she was up to secret tricks.

Catherine, as a married woman, was supposed to produce an heir almost instantly. When time passed and she did not, Elizabeth increased her senseless and vicious restraints. Catherine was forbidden to romp with her maidens; and a strict, unfriendly governess was put in charge of her. Every move Catherine made was watched and every word she said reported. Her governess warned everyone who came near her that if he said more than "yes" or "no" it would be reported to the Empress that Catherine was plotting with him. Elizabeth's spies watched her through keyholes and burst in on her in the middle of the night.

Both Catherine and Peter were scolded incessantly, like naughty children. They were not even allowed to go for a walk or take a bath without permission. If either one made a friend, they would soon hear that he had been ordered suddenly to Astrakhan or banished to Siberia or shut up in the fortress on a trumped-up charge.

The truth was that Elizabeth, fearful and suspicious, was losing her grip on reality.

As a young girl the Empress had been beautiful, warm-hearted and picturesque; and she still retained vivid traces of her youth. To the dazzled fourteen-year-old Elizabeth had seemed at first view a magnificent goddess. But as the Empress grew older, she became jealous of youth, terrified of plots against her throne, superstitious to a hysterical degree and increasingly self-indulgent. In a seizure of terror, she would banish a member of the court to Siberia and confiscate his property. Even if he were found to be innocent, he could never again regain his position because Elizabeth was afraid to admit she was wrong. Incurably soft-hearted, the sentimental Empress would weep as she signed warrants against innocent people, who were then beaten to death, mutilated or banished. In a fit of hatred against those who were young and beautiful, she once ordered all the ladies of the court to shave off their hair and don ugly black wigs, so they would not be different from her. (The merchants' wives wore black wigs, too, at this time to imitate the court. But they did not cut off their hair, and as a result their heads looked enormous.)

One day the Empress ordered two young ladies before her and, in the presence of the entire court, cut off their curled bangs. The ladies said afterwards that the Empress had been so angry that she had cut off a little skin along with the hair.

Those nearest the Empress—particularly Catherine and Peter—suffered most from her caprices, her fears and her possessive tyranny. Catherine had no friends, and she turned finally to her mother. Johanna understood her daughter's wretchedness. For the first time in her life she was sympathetic.

But Johanna had got herself in trouble with her ceaseless intrigues. Elizabeth was notoriously capricious with her favorites, who came and went overnight. Johanna had involved herself with a faction of the court which was no longer in favor. She so irritated Elizabeth with her secret maneuverings that the Empress peremptorily ordered her to leave Russia.

Catherine, who had kept herself entirely aloof from intrigue, was desolate to see her mother go. Now she was quite alone in the treacherous quagmire of the Russian court.

In the first year of her marriage she grew very thin. She cried often, suffered from sleeplessness and had a succession of headaches, toothaches and colds. The once-healthy girl, who despised imaginary physical ailments, had to use twelve handkerchiefs a day for her running nose!

She became timid and reserved and used the utmost deference in speaking to everyone. Once someone gave her a little dog, and she burst into tears. She never expected a mark of friendliness or kindness.

Shortly after her marriage, Catherine received word that her father had died. She wept inconsolably and became ill. Elizabeth, annoyed at her grief, sent a message to Catherine through her governess.

"Your father was no king," the woman said unkindly, "and the loss is not so great."

"It is true that my father was no king," said Catherine with sudden dignity. "But he was after all my father. I may assume it is no crime to mourn for him."

She was not allowed to write personal letters, and even on the death of her father she could not write a note to her mother. When she received a letter, it had already been opened and read. She had to send it immediately to the College of Foreign Affairs, where it would be officially answered. She could not even suggest what was to be written.

One day during a court presentation a foreign count secretly thrust a letter into her hand. It was from her mother, desperately anxious because Catherine no longer wrote to her. A few days later, at a concert, Catherine was standing near the orchestra. The musician who played bass said, without turning his head, "The count charged me to give you his respects, and begs you to let him have your answer during the next concert."

Catherine had neither pen, paper nor ink. She could not keep them in her room because her governess would have asked why she needed them. She had trinkets brought to her, pretending that she wanted to buy some gifts. Among other things she picked out a fountain pen and had the servant fill it with ink. Behind locked doors, late at night, she tore the blank pages out of several books and wrote a letter to her mother. At the next concert she slipped the letter into the musician's pocket as he was playing.

Unhappy and terribly bored, Catherine turned to reading as her only solace. At first she read light and romantic fantasies. But as she grew more thoughtful and critical of those around her, her reading grew more serious. One winter and spring she read a formidable history of Germany in nine volumes. She discovered the works of Voltaire, and found the free-thinking, sharp-tongued Frenchman much to her liking. The innocent Grand Duchess, surrounded by luxury and wife of the heir to a powerful medieval autocracy, became an ardent disciple of the apostle of freedom, justice and equality. "In truth," she said later, "he was my teacher. Or, better said, his works have formed my mind and spirit."

She seldom laid down her books. In the morning she awoke early and read until time to dress. While her hair was being dressed, she continued to read. At eleven-thirty she had to meet her ladies in the reception room, where the conversation was stilted and careful. At twelve they joined the Empress and had dinner, a long, formal meal at which no one said anything interesting. Catherine read all afternoon, until six, which was the hour for promenading and refreshment—again with the same tedious company. At eight the same people took supper together; and at ten the evening was over, and she could return to her books.

As Catherine strengthened herself during these difficult years, her husband deteriorated. Peter, as a man, was no longer simply childish—he was becoming mentally deranged. His passion for military maneuvers was now an obsession. Once Catherine, entering his room, saw a dead rat on a gallows. Peter told her, quite seriously, that a military court martial and execution had just taken place. His tutors kept such a strict watch over him that he could not play with his dolls except late at night, in Catherine's room with all the doors locked. He would put them through military exercise, oblivious of his wife, until two or three in the morning. Forbidden to train his lackeys he trained Cather-

ine in soldierly exercise. Good-humoredly she allowed
him to march her back and forth across the room, and
would stand guard at his door with a musket at her
shoulder. She was amused at the thought that she was
acquiring from her imbecilic husband a military polish
as fine as that of the best-drilled grenadier. Sometimes
they played cards. But Catherine took care to make
mistakes so that Peter would win. If he lost, he flew into
a tantrum and reviled her in the worst language.

In fact he knew almost no other way to talk. Who-
ever befriended him was jailed or sent away, so the
lowest lackeys were his only companions, and their obscenities became his only language. He could not even
dine with the lords and ladies. Elizabeth had banished him from the dinner table because he used foul
oaths.

Besides his unbalanced passion for military maneuvers, Peter had another, more dangerous obsession.
This was a deep hatred for everything Russian and admiration for everything German. He dreamed and
talked constantly of Holstein, the little German duchy
where he had spent his childhood. In his mind it had
become a rosy-hued paradise in which he had per-
formed unparalleled acts of heroism. He boasted that
he had, at the head of a battalion, successfully driven
off a far larger Danish force which was assailing his beloved country. Peter had left Holstein forever when
he was fifteen years old, but he told this impossible
tale so often that he truly believed it. Still Duke of
Holstein, he was expected to handle its affairs. But he
was unable to pay attention to serious matters for more
than five minutes at a time. So he handed over the
ministerial papers to his wife. This was fine training

for the Grand Duchess. She handled the affairs of his duchy with straight-thinking good sense, while Peter played with his dolls and dreamed great dreams of Prussian heroism.

The deity of his private paradise was King Frederick II of Prussia. This worldly monarch was embarrassed by the expressions of devotion addressed to him by the silly Grand Duke. He laughed at Peter and said to his friends, "I am his Dulcinea. He has never seen me, and has fallen in love with me, like Don Quixote." But Frederick was astute, and he realized that this neurotic Don Quixote was an important ally. After all he would one day be Czar of Russia. He sent useful advice to the Grand Duke, and tried to temper his off-balance enthusiasms.

Besides military training Peter had only two occupations. He liked to play the violin, but he played it very badly. And he trained dogs. When he had tired of training Catherine, she would go into her room and close the door between them. But she could not shut out the sounds of the discordant scraping of the violin. This alternated with the terrible howling of five or six dogs, which he trained by beating them with a stick. Catherine tried to read, but was near to screaming with exasperation.

"No one is as unhappy as I," she thought desperately. "Except maybe the dogs."

But she had a strange, motherly sympathy for her pathetic husband. She humored him and was unendingly patient. With adult wisdom she realized that most of his peculiar behavior came from ill treatment. She knew he was mentally deficient but did not believe he had any evil in him.

His wife, in fact, was the only person in the Russian court who paid any attention to Peter at all.

Difficult and tedious as Catherine's daily life at court was, it was still better than accompanying the Empress on her many trips. She made Catherine and Peter go with her on pilgrimages to holy shrines, to wonder-working wooden virgins that were said to shed real tears, and to uncorrupted corpses of saints, kept in dry underground caves and believed to perform miracles. Three priests always accompanied the Empress. They were her cavaliers and squired her gallantly to balls and operas, when they were not all praying and fasting. Catherine tried to imagine Pastor Wagner taking her to a masquerade. Though she did not often smile these days, the thought made her laugh.

Every few weeks Elizabeth moved the entire court to another of her many palaces—for no reason except that she was restless. Everyone except the Empress was extremely uncomfortable on these trips. She required the post houses for herself and her retinue. Catherine and Peter and their small company often had to sleep on the floor, in rooms where bread was baked and where the stove was going all night, filling the room with smoke. If there were no rooms to be had, tents were put up. The tents always came too late. When they arrived late at night, they were put up just anywhere. Once they were stretched in a place where there were six inches of water.

Many of the palaces where the court stayed were decrepit and crumbling. Once the house in which Catherine was sleeping fell down in the middle of the night, nearly burying her. She was carried out by one of the guards just as the house slipped from its foundations and crashed down a steep hill. At the next place they stayed, the walls were tested. It was found that the beams were so decayed that they would not have stood another month. So the court lived in one lower wing and ate in a tent which was put up in the middle of the courtyard.

Even the grand Summer Palace at St. Petersburg was designed in such a primitive manner that an ambassador, walking in at the front door for an audience with the Empress, would meet, coming out of the same door, a lackey carrying a chamber pot.

At every stopping place the ladies and gentlemen of the court did exactly the same things they had done at all the other palaces. In the daytime one would see in the gardens ladies in heavy, full-skirted silk or velvet dresses, embroidered with pearls, their hair powdered or dyed, and dressed with diamonds, their faces painted like actresses'. They were accompanied by highly perfumed court fops with their hair carefully dressed in pigeon-wing curls, wearing brilliantly embroidered coats and breeches with jeweled buckles at the knees. The gentlemen would swing the ladies in broad swings, play feather ball or idly throw bread to the swans, whispering gossip all the while.

In the evening they danced and played cards. Cards were indispensable because there was no conversation. Slander was considered wit and intrigue took the place of wisdom. Half the court could neither read nor write, and art and science were unknown.

Catherine disliked card playing, and she was not allowed to do anything else. She had always enjoyed physical exercise, and she would have loved to gallop

on horseback across the flower-filled northern meadows. But Elizabeth insisted it was bad for her. She
could not even take a walk alone.

In her enforced idleness the Grand Duchess had
plenty of time to observe the habits and daily life of
nobles and peasants. She had loved St. Petersburg and
Moscow at first sight. At second sight she saw in what
slipshod fashion the people lived behind the pretty
painted walls and the façade of ostentation. In St. Petersburg the only stone houses were on three paved
streets. Beyond them stretched muddy, unpaved lanes
lined with ugly, barrack-like houses of rough logs.
Even the beautiful stone houses, designed by Italian
architects for a southern climate, were uncomfortable
and inconvenient. Because the houses had no cellars,
the floors were uneven, cracked and always damp. The
furniture was poor and sparse, and the walls were
whitewashed or hung with cheap paper, spotted with
mildew.

In Moscow Catherine was even more surprised by
the sloth and indolence in which the rich gentry lived.
One would see a lavishly gowned lady drive forth from
a great court filled with heaps of dirt and trash. Her
decrepit carriage, extravagantly gilded, was drawn by
six shabby horses with dirty harnesses or even ropes.
The lady's lackeys, dressed in handsome livery, were
rude and unkempt, their hair uncombed, their hands
dirty. The bright-painted mansions which had impressed Catherine on that far distant snowy night were
mostly of wood and rotting at their very foundations.
Their courtyards were mud holes, their gardens un-
tended fields.

Peter also played the violin and trained dogs.

The gentlemen of Moscow gambled day and night. The ladies adorned themselves eternally and paid no attention to household duties. There were so many house servants that the ladies had nothing else to do. Sometimes a house would have thirty to forty maids employed only on needlework. One lady had two maids whose only duty was to read to her as she fell asleep. They had to continue reading for hours after she slept; if they stopped, she would wake up in a rage and have them whipped. Another old woman who had lost her hair and wanted no one to know it, kept a slave in a cage in her room for five years. She let him see no one and fed him through the bars. Twice a day he was let out to arrange her wig.

Not only were the gentry of Moscow lazy; they were also cruel. Every grand house had its pillory, chains, whips and other instruments of torture ready for the least offense by a servant. Catherine was deeply shocked by the cruelty of master to slave, and even more so by the thought that one man could own another.

And she was horrified to the depths of her still-Protestant soul by the mummery that passed for religion. The people, nobles and peasants alike, were not so much religious as superstitious. The priests were incredibly boorish and ignorant. There were more churches in Russia than anywhere else in the world. Their tall, slender spires and clusters of onion-shaped domes were beautifully gilded and painted. Inside were walls and floors of intricate mosaics, much incense, hundreds of candles and bright-painted ikons and figures. The service was very long, sometimes lasting all day. It consisted of a continuous succession of kneeling, prostrating full length on the floor and crossing oneself. In fact the congregation was so seldom off the floor that no seats were provided.

The priests who conducted the services had long beards, hair down to their shoulders and flowing robes of the most exquisitely delicate embroidery, encrusted with gold, pearls and precious stones. These had usually been made by the ladies of the parish (or more likely their maids) as covering for a dead person; afterwards they were given to the church.

But imposing as they looked, priests were considered among the lowest class. At a nobleman's table the priest ate with the footmen. Many could not read; most of them were intemperate. On certain days of the year priests in the country made a tour of their parishes demanding eggs, butter, flax or chickens. One would often see them at the end of the day, either lying drunk and asleep at the bottom of the cart or singing merrily as they drove it.

Holy ikons were bartered on every street corner. These ikons were the peasants' most precious and revered possessions. They were appealed to on entering a house, consulted and prayed to many times a day, scolded and praised according to whether things had gone well or ill. At night the people placed their mattresses so that their heads, not their feet, faced the holy image. When an ikon was worn out, it was thrown into the river. Then it was bad luck. If it came ashore, anyone who saw it must push it back into the moving water again.

This superstition, ignorance and cruelty in her adopted country horrified Catherine in the first years.

Wretched, frightened and absorbed in her own troubles, she felt that everything around her looked sour.

But gradually her natural cheerfulness came back, and she began again to take pleasure in her surroundings. And she learned about her country—from observing, from talking to people and above all from reading. She came to understand that Russia was only a short time away from the Dark Ages. Less than seventy years before, Russia had been in the same state as Europe in the eleventh century. She marveled at the quickness of the Russians, their eagerness to learn, their natural skill. She ceased condemning their ignorance and thought instead of ways to improve them. Her mind full of the reforms of the French enlightened philosophers, the serious young Grand Duchess began to plan for the future of "her people."

As the years passed, Catherine lost her timidity and acquired a regal air. She learned how to assert herself against injustice. And her warm-hearted friendliness overflowed the barriers of solitude and boredom. First she made friends with her servants and maids-in-waiting. They adored her because she was easy with them and gave them presents. Sometimes she forgot her new seriousness and danced, skipped and mimicked hilariously as in the days when she had been "young"—at twenty it seemed strange to her that she had grown so old. But she was careful never to confide in them.

Slowly and cautiously she began to make friends at court. In the welter of intrigue and scandal, Catherine was respected. She never said anything cruel; she would not listen to evil gossip, and she never betrayed a confidence. Everyone trusted her. In a court dominated by a drunken, capricious and wanton empress,

Catherine was regarded as a tower of good sense. More and more foreign ambassadors and government officials turned to her for help and advice. Everyone was grateful that the imbecilic, half-mad heir had a wife who was sane, serious and trustworthy. If she was not happy, Catherine finally knew that she had friends.

In 1754, after nine years of marriage, Catherine produced a male heir. The baby, christened Paul Petrovich, was snatched away by the possessive Elizabeth at the moment of his birth. Catherine was only allowed to see him for a few minutes at a time, and she was shocked at the way he was treated by his devoted nurse, the Empress. He lay in a hot dark room, entirely wrapped in flannel, in a crib made of black fox fur and covered with a padded satin cover. Over this was another cover, of heavy red velvet lined with fox fur. His little face and his whole bed were wet with sweat. Elizabeth hovered over him with tense possessiveness. The baby seemed timid and over-sensitive. He would tremble violently at a sound, and the Empress would snatch him up and murmur hysterical endearments.

Catherine was disgusted, but helpless. Forced to give up all claim to her son, she soon lost interest in him.

But the birth of the child gave Catherine unexpected freedom. Again she was in the good graces of the Empress. She was allowed to receive her friends openly, to write letters. She did not abuse her new freedom. She continued to educate herself and at this time started correspondences with learned and witty men all over Europe. Voltaire was her favorite and most frequent correspondent. Perhaps more important politically was her correspondence with Frederick II, of whom she had been so in awe when she was a shy fourteen-year-old on her way to Russia. This King's mind was as quick as those of the philosophers with whom he surrounded himself. His letters not only entertained Catherine, they contained good political advice. The wily King knew that this was an important friendship. This agile-minded and sensible young woman would undoubtedly be a power when her witless husband came to the throne.

Catherine even began writing plays. These were usually biting satires on sentimentality, hypocrisy and superstition—those traits in Elizabeth and Peter from which she had suffered so much. She had no hope that her plays would ever be produced; she dared not even let anyone read them. But they were an escape for her pent-up feelings. Always self-controlled, cheerful and friendly in public, Catherine gave herself the luxury of hating her life in private.

Catherine's husband, meanwhile, was continuing on his spiral of self-destruction. The year after his son was born, he suddenly stopped playing with toy soldiers and imported some real ones from his beloved Holstein. The regiment of Holsteiners was thoroughly hated by the Russian guard with whom it was quartered. "These accursed Germans are all sold to the King of Prussia," they said. Besides, they complained, the Holsteiners were quarrelsome, took up too much room and ate too much. Peter had always been despised by the Russian guard. Now they had an active grievance against him.

He made himself even more unpopular by refusing to go to the Greek Orthodox Church. He had private Lutheran services for himself—although he was not religious, only afraid of the devil.

His worst stupidity was to allow himself to become involved in a clumsy plot against Elizabeth. The plan, which failed, was to put Elizabeth in a convent and turn the throne over to her heir. Though she had no direct proof of Peter's guilt, she suspected him. Instead of punishing him the Empress pettishly refused to allow him to see her any more. "My nephew is an imbecile!" she cried angrily. "Let the devil fetch him." Peter raved against her impotently, and retaliated by refusing to go to the steam bath when he was told to.

The malicious absurdity of this quarrel irritated Catherine. With stern reserve she withheld herself from any part in it.

With the failure of the plot and his growing unpopularity, Peter became wildly anxious to have the crown, and fearful that it might slip out of his grasp. He was jealous of his wife, with her sureness and her regal manner and her many friends. She was unfailingly good-humored with him and was the only one who tried to protect him against the dislike of those who surrounded him. But he began to fear her, knowing she was a superior being. From fear it was a short step to hatred. Catherine appeared to him as a menace.

The personal life of the Grand Duchess was simple, even frugal. But her generous extravagance toward others had already become a byword all over Europe.

By the end of 1761 Catherine was so much in debt that she did not have enough money to order a new dress for Christmas.

But she did not need a new dress. For on that Christmas Day the Empress Elizabeth died. She fell in a fit, while feasting, with a glass of cherry brandy at her lips.

The witless, vindictive Grand Duke, Catherine's husband and enemy, became Emperor Peter III.

5 The Revolution

Peter was beside himself with joy. As the court assembled in the cathedral a few hours after Elizabeth's death, to give him the oath of allegiance, the new Emperor grinned, made silly faces and babbled gaily.

"A ridiculous harlequin!" whispered the French ambassador to the English ambassador.

"The new Emperor is quite mad," answered the Englishman.

At Elizabeth's funeral procession Peter, wearing a long black mourning robe, walked directly behind the black carriage containing the coffin. He was followed by his wife and the other members of the court according to rank. Peter was in high good humor and decided to play a joke. He lingered behind the mourning carriage and allowed it to get about seventy yards ahead of him. Then he ran to catch up with it. The dignified elderly chamberlains who carried the train of his black robe could not keep up with him and had to let go. The wind billowed the long train high, and Peter was delighted. He repeated this "joke" several times, and the procession got farther and farther behind. Finally someone had to send a message up to the front, and the mourning carriage halted until the rest could catch up.

The Emperor started his reign with a series of orders, some of which were ridiculous, some dangerous. He ordered that the gentlemen of the court could hunt ravens and other birds in the streets of St. Petersburg; also that they could shoot on sight all dogs found near the palace.

He pledged allegiance to Frederick II of Prussia and signed an eternal peace with him. At a banquet celebrating this peace Peter grandiloquently proposed a "three times three" toast: to Peter III of Russia, George III of England and Frederick III of Prussia. Someone pointed out to him that Frederick was only II. Peter did not listen, but ordered fireworks over the river Neva in an elaborate design of "3 × 3."

He started to Germanize the army—replaced the horse guards and other honor regiments with Helsteiners, instituted German military drill, took away the long warm coats of the soldiers and put them into tight German uniforms. Every Russian soldier, from general to private, grumbled at these orders. The Russian army was fiercely proud of its traditions.

He ordered his generals to prepare for a war against Denmark. Russia had no grievance against Denmark. But Holstein had because Denmark held a few square miles of Holstein land. At this command the army came dangerously close to mutiny. Peter, afraid of his soldiers, made his uncle, Prince George of Holstein, generalissimo—a position which by custom should have been held by the Emperor himself. Prince George was leery of his new command.

"Your Majesty must have a second army," he said, "to make that under my command advance."

Frederick II had got more than he bargained for in his new ally. He counseled Peter to give up the war against Denmark and go slowly in confiscating church lands. But the mad Emperor would not listen even to his idol. He careened down his crazy path, ordered wholesale arrests at court, indulged in orgies of drinking at every meal, quarreled and ranted against everyone. Now that he was emperor he did not have to restrict himself to torturing servants. Favorites were often beaten in front of the entire court. Narishkin, the gay courtier who had met Catherine when she first arrived in Russia, was cudgeled with a stick by the demented monarch in the presence of the diplomatic corps and about a hundred spectators, men and women, at a festival.

In the beginning Peter did nothing to Catherine, and she kept out of his way. Her influence at court was large, and the Emperor was afraid of her. But she knew that if she so much as lifted a finger he would have her arrested. From the day of his accession to the throne he talked openly of divorcing her. But nothing was done about it, for Catherine gave him no cause.

Immediately after Elizabeth's death, Princess Dashkov, a close friend of Catherine, came to her and said, "Give the order and we will place you on the throne."

"For God's sake, do nothing foolish!" Oddly, Catherine was still sympathetic with her husband. "His mind is no longer just right," she continued. "But he does not have a bad heart. He has not in the whole kingdom a worse enemy than himself. All will happen as Providence wills."

As she kept aloof from all intrigue, she also refused to take a hand in the administration of the state. She wore heavy black mourning draperies and appeared at no court functions except on the most necessary formal occasions.

But Peter seemed bent on alienating her. Five months after his accession, at a royal banquet, he proposed a toast to the imperial family. Catherine pledged him but did not rise from her seat. Peter sent a messenger to ask why she did not stand. She replied politely that she was a member of the imperial family, and it would not be fitting for her to rise and toast herself.

Peter stood up and shouted roughly down the table, "*Dura!*" This was a coarse expression, meaning "stupid woman," which was used only in the most vulgar street arguments. Catherine's face reddened, her eyes filled with tears, and she left the table without a word.

This was the first time her husband had dared to insult her openly. The next day she learned that right after the banquet Peter had issued an order for her arrest. He had been persuaded to withdraw it. But Catherine knew she was no longer safe.

She realized also that Russia was seething with anger against the monarch. At any moment the country might boil over into revolution, bloodshed and anarchy. Catherine knew her popularity. And she was quite certain that she could be a good ruler.

She made up her mind and called her friends around her.

Catherine had five devoted admirers, the young Orlov brothers. All officers of the Russian guard, they lived in the barracks. They assured her that all the soldiers of the capital were on her side. The young Empress, natural, friendly and courageous, had always been popular with the Russian soldiers. Even the lowest private knew her kind smile and her merry eye. Many of them fancied themselves in love with her. In fact, one was truly so; though discreet and conscious of his lowly position, he kept absolute silence. That was a very youthful lieutenant, Gregory Potemkin of the Horse Guards, an honor regiment. He had been intended for the church and had been a devoutly good student. But deep as his faith was, his character was vivacious and violent. His father had decided he would be better off as a soldier. But he never lost his passionate mysticism. When he saw Catherine, cheerful and heroic in the midst of loneliness and cruelty, he fell immediately in love with her. The spiritual fervor that had once turned him toward religion now centered entirely on her. Though he loved in silence he responded eagerly when invited to join the revolution.

The decision was made that the guards would mutiny, arrest Peter on the grounds of incompetence and place Catherine on the throne. Princess Dashkov and two other members of the court helped in the planning of the coup. In fact, thirty or forty officers and several thousand soldiers knew about it. Yet there was, incredibly, no leakage.

Peter had been emperor for just six months. June 27, 1762, was the day before his name day. The name day—celebration of the saint for whom one was named—was a more important occasion in Russia than a birthday. Peter had planned a national holiday for his. The day after it the Russian army was to march against Denmark. All Russia was fuming and growling like an active volcano.

The night of June 27th Catherine was at one of the country palaces outside St. Petersburg. She was sleeping by herself in a little summer house called Mon Plaisir, on the edge of the blue Gulf of Finland.

Before dawn a man climbed in her window and called softly, "*Matushka*, Little Mother, wake up. You must leave here immediately!"

Catherine leaped up. She saw that the intruder was Alexei Orlov, leader of the Orlov clan. "But it was not planned for this day, Alexei!"

"They have arrested one of the lieutenants. If they torture him, he may tell everything. Then it is all over. Come!" He vanished into the dark garden.

Catherine's festival dress was laid out ready to wear. But she put on instead her old black mourning dress which she had worn since the death of Elizabeth. She slipped out of the house into the intense pre-dawn blackness. There were a few stars, and she could hear the soft whisper of the waves at the foot of her terrace. Immediately she was lost in the dark maze of the immense palace gardens. But, high-spirited and adventurous, she felt now that nothing could frighten her. After an hour of wandering she found the high-way. Alexei was waiting there silently beside an open carriage with one horse. He handed her in, and they galloped down the dusty road toward St. Petersburg.

They had not gone a mile when the horse caught his foot in a hole and fell. Catherine jumped out of the carriage. "Come, we will walk," she cried. She hoisted up her heavy black skirts and set off briskly in the dim dawn light. They had walked more than a mile when they met a peasant's cart. Alexei lifted Catherine in, seized the reins from the surprised far-mer, turned the cart around and whipped the horse into a gallop.

They had one more encounter—Catherine's hair-dresser, on his way to the palace to fix her hair for the celebration. Catherine looked at her dusty black skirts, at the determined, stern soldier beside her, at the rough-hewn boards of the peasant cart. She laughed and told the hairdresser he could turn around and go home. He would not be needed that day.

At seven in the morning they came to St. Petersburg. Catherine went to regimental headquarters, where the soldiers fell at her feet, kissed her hands and the hem of her dress and called her their savior. Two of them led forward a priest with a cross. The priest blessed her; then all the soldiers knelt and took the oath of allegiance.

She went from regiment to regiment all over the city, receiving everywhere the same ecstatic welcome. When she came to the horse guards, the handsomely dressed soldiers marched their horses in a parade of homage. Suddenly one of the horses wheeled out of

"Madame," he said, "you have no plume in your hat."

line and approached Catherine. On the strong, dark face of its young rider were written a searching intelligence, unbending pride and almost unwilling admiration for the new Queen. Half morose, half adoring, he looked her straight in the eye.

"Madame," he said, "you have no plume in your hat. Permit me to offer you mine." He tore the plume from his hat and presented it to Catherine. Then he turned as suddenly as he had come and rejoined his regiment, his eyes straight ahead.

"Who is he?" whispered Catherine to Gregory Orlov, who stood next to her.

"Lieutenant Potemkin," said Orlov with a frown.

"Had he a part in the revolution?"

Unwillingly her escort answered, "He was among the officers who helped us to plan the coup." Catherine knew why he was sulky. Gregory Orlov, one of the five faithful brothers who had organized her revolution, had openly stated his desire to become emperor. He wanted no rivals in his courting of the young Queen he had helped to the throne. She gave him a dazzling smile and kept her thoughts to herself. There would be time enough later to tell him there would be no emperor during her reign.

But she remembered the sullen, handsome face and the gallant gesture of Lieutenant Potemkin.

By the time she came to the palace, the streets were full of people laughing and cheering. In the palace she gathered some of the court into a makeshift council. A manifesto was drawn up declaring Peter unfit to rule and naming Catherine empress.

In the middle of the meeting, Peter's chancellor came in. In formal language he reproached Catherine for her flight. He told her the monarch was angry, and had ordered her immediate arrest.

"Have you seen the people in the streets?" asked Catherine. "I am the ruler now."

The chancellor bowed low. "Forgive me, your Imperial Majesty," he said. "I came only to do my duty." And forthwith he took the oath of allegiance to her. Two more of Peter's favorites came, offered a token complaint and declared themselves Catherine's courtiers. Peter had no friend.

When Peter learned that his wife had left secretly in the night, he fell into panic. He rushed to Mon Plaisir, hunted for her everywhere, even under the bed, and questioned the servants angrily. Then he turned to his people and asked what he should do. Everyone had a different plan, but Peter followed none of them. Abjectly weak and indecisive, he paced up and down in the garden, and then suddenly demanded that dinner should be served. After dinner he called for a galley and two pleasure yachts and said he would go and take Cronstadt, a nearby Russian seaport. When the pitiful little flotilla reached Cronstadt late in the afternoon, it was stopped by one officer. Although this young soldier had no authority at all he stood on the sea wall and shouted, "There is no Emperor! Move off or we fire!" Peter ordered his ships to turn around, and they sailed back to the palace. There he got word that all the Russian regiments had deserted him.

He sat down and wrote two letters to Catherine. In the first he asked to be allowed to return to Holstein. In the second he offered to renounce the throne and kingdom for his life.

Peter III had given up.

In the meantime Catherine was preparing to arrest him. She asked her council to make her Colonel of the Guards. Then she borrowed a uniform from one of the lieutenants, mounted a white horse and placed herself at the head of 10,000 soldiers.

The whole city turned out to see her go. In a fever of exultation they cheered their beautiful young Queen. She had a garland of oak leaves around her shining black hair. Her face was pale, but her eyes sparkled with vivid excitement. Tall and gallant and proud, she rode her big horse as easily as a soldier.

In a corner of her mind was little Fike, riding on a pillow and dreaming of this day.

Peter's pitiful, abject letters reached her as she neared the palace grounds. She dispatched Alexei Orlov with an answering letter demanding a formal resignation. He galloped to the palace while Catherine waited with her army at the gates.

The tall, stern, silent soldier stood in Peter's doorway with Catherine's letter in his hand. Peter stared at him with insane horror. All at once it seemed that the dread military symbol of his childhood terrors had come to life. He cringed and cowered and babbled piteously and said he would do whatever anyone wanted him to. Alexei directed him to take pen and paper, and dictated his resignation. Trembling, Peter wrote:

"In the short period of my reign as autocrat of the Russian Empire I have realized its hardships and burdens, to which my powers are not equal, so that neither as autocrat nor in any other way can I rule the Russian Empire. Thus I perceived that inward changes were leading to the destruction of its safety and would necessarily bring lasting disgrace to me. I have therefore taken counsel with myself and herewith solemnly declare without hatred and without compulsion, not merely to the Russian Empire but to all the world, that I renounce the sovereignty of the Russian Empire for my whole life. As long as I live I will never reign over the Russian Empire as autocrat, nor in any other way, and I will never myself nor with anyone's help strive for it. I swear this sincerely

and without hypocrisy before God and the whole
world. This entire abdication I have written and signed
with my own hand. The 29th day of June in the year
1762. Peter."

When he had finished, the miserable little man
put his head on the desk and sobbed like a child.

The revolution was over. In twenty-four hours, without a single drop of blood shed, the Russian throne
had passed from its legal owner to an obscure German
princess who had no right to it either by blood or
heritage.

The next day, June 30th, the Empress, at the head of
her troops, marched back to St. Petersburg in the
early morning, amid the wild jubilation of the multi-
tudes. She rode into the courtyard of the palace. There
a courtier met her, bearing in his arms an eight-year-
old bundle of misery, her shivering little son Paul,
still in his nightgown, his face puffed with sleepiness.
Catherine was momentarily taken aback. Fear and revulsion swept over her at this, her most glorious hour,
as she contemplated her miserable heir.

Paul had a striking resemblance to his father, both
in looks and manner; and every time his mother saw
him she involuntarily recoiled, remembering the long
years, now so happily ended, when she had been tied
to an imbecile and victimized by a jealous empress.
During Elizabeth's lifetime Paul had been under the
constant care of that hysterically possessive woman.
His mother had been allowed only brief glimpses of
him. Eight years of Elizabeth's stifling attention had
been enough to ruin little Paul, who had been weak
to begin with. In the six months since the Empress'

death, Catherine had tried to establish some contact with her son, and to overcome the strange reluctance with which she viewed this morbidly sensitive, fearful child.

Catherine had mothered her two sick brothers; she had mothered her weak-minded husband. She was naturally affectionate and sympathetic toward those weaker than she. But Paul repelled her. He was not only weak, he was extremely unpleasant; and even at this young age his character was violent. Unhappy and frightened herself, Catherine had been unable to see that Paul, even with his fierce and ugly moods, was a pathetic little boy. Elizabeth had spoiled and coddled him, given him her fanatical mysticism and obsessive superstitions, taught him jealousy and capriciousness. But she had been the only one who cared about him. With her death his prop was gone. He was afraid of this regal, sure, beautiful woman who looked at him so coldly and had never been a mother to him.

Sternly Catherine suppressed her thoughts. She had usurped a throne. Her son was her only claim to legality. The blood of Peter the Great ran in his veins. She dismounted, greeted Paul tenderly and held him up in her arms.

"Here is my heir," she said. The mob cheered deafeningly as Catherine lifted the trembling child to her horse. Together they rode to the cathedral, where a solemn service of thanksgiving was held. All day long the cannons roared and the bells rang, as on her wedding day. But Catherine was no longer an unhappy, lonely bride. The new Queen, regal but glowing with friendliness, greeted everyone who wished to see her. The gates of the palace were thrown open and all day the soldiers tramped over the teakwood and mosaic floors and the magnificent Persian carpets.

Catherine had not slept since the beginning of her revolution. Finally she fell into bed in exhaustion. She slept for three hours. Then, for the second time in three days, she was awakened by a man coming into her room. It was a captain of one of the regiments.

"Little Mother, forgive me. Our soldiers are terribly drunk. A hussar has just been running about and crying out, 'To arms! Thirty thousand Prussians are coming and wish to take our Mother!' They all seized their weapons and are now coming here to see if you are all right. They say they have not seen you for the last three hours. They will not listen to their leaders."

As he spoke, Catherine heard the shouting, jostling soldiers approaching. She hastily wrapped herself in a dressing gown and went to the door. The first soldiers brandished their weapons in her face and shouted that they were ready to die for her.

Catherine stood tall and straight, her black hair falling around her shoulders. "I know you would die for me," she said quietly, as if she were talking to children. "I thank you all, my brothers. As you see, I am perfectly safe. You must obey your officers. Now go to bed." Fervently the soldiers wished her good night and good health. They left as peacefully as lambs, turning back frequently as long as they could still see her.

Peter had been taken to Ropsha, a small, unfortified country palace. There he was to be kept for a few days until arrangements could be made to send him back to Holstein. He was unhappy at Ropsha. The soldiers, who hated him, kept him confined in a small, dim bedroom with green curtains which were always closed. There the wretched creature, who had never been able to stay more than an hour in one place, paced back and forth all day in an agony of nervousness. He wrote pathetic, begging letters to Catherine, asking for his own bed, his violin, his dog and his Negro servant. These were given to him. But he was still desperate in his confinement.

While he suffered, his soldier guards were bored and restless. They drank all day and played cards. And Alexei Orlov, Peter's chief jailer, wrote his own letters to Catherine:

"Little Mother, Gracious Empress. We all wish you health for countless years. Our monster has grown very sick and has had an unexpected attack of colic. And I am afraid that he might die tonight, and fear still more that he might live. The first fear I have because he chatters pure nonsense; the second, because he is really dangerous, and often speaks as if he had his former position."

For four days Peter was sick with colic and diarrhea. On the fifth day, weak and still fevered, he was allowed to come out of his jail for dinner. He could not eat but immediately started drinking. His guards also drank heavily, and the meal degenerated into a drunken orgy.

The next morning, July 6th, a messenger brought Catherine another letter from Alexei:

"Little Mother, Merciful Empress! How shall I tell you, how describe, what has happened? You will not believe your faithful servant, but before God I will speak the truth. Little Mother! I am ready to die, but I do not know myself how the mischief came about. We are lost if you do not have mercy on us. Little Mother, he tarries no longer on this earth. But no one would have believed it, and how could we have thought of laying hands upon him! But Empress, the misfortune has happened! He fell into a quarrel at table with Prince Feodor; we could not separate them, and already he was no more. We ourselves could not remember what we had done, but we are all guilty to the very last one and deserving of death. I have made my confession and there is nothing to investigate. Pardon, or else command quickly that an end be made! We have angered you and hurled our souls to eternal destruction."

Catherine read the letter in silence, her face strained and paler than usual. "He is gone," she said at last and fell into a faint. Afterwards she had convulsions, and it was thought that she would die.

When she recovered and remembered what had happened, she shed bitter tears. "My glory has departed," she said. "Posterity will never forgive me for this unintended crime."

She immediately ordered that Peter's body should be dissected. The doctors found evidence of inflammation of the intestines and a fit of apoplexy. They also reported that his heart was unusually small and quite withered. Alexei Orlov and the others were officially cleared of all blame for his death.

For the rest of her life Catherine maintained an unbroken silence on the subject of the death of her husband. Neither she nor anyone else—except perhaps Alexei Orlov—would ever know exactly what had happened.

6 Benevolent Despot

When Catherine became empress, she was thirty-three years old and at the peak of her beauty and her mental powers. Her soft black hair was naturally wavy and her skin dazzling white. She had large expressive blue eyes with very long lashes, a Greek nose and a mouth which curled naturally into a smile. Tall and graceful, she had beautifully rounded arms and shoulders, long, lovely hands and an agile grace in walking. A pleasant voice, a joyous laugh and a temperament gay and easy-going made her beloved by all who met her.

But this Queen who adored wit and laughter could

also clarify the meaning of a complicated legal document. She could follow with perfect understanding the vast network of intrigue which passed for foreign policy in eighteenth-century Europe. Her mind was sharper than any of those around her, and she had an immediate, almost uncanny grasp of character. Suavity did not deceive her, and flattery left her entirely cold.

In her eighteen years in Russia, Catherine had learned a great deal about the history and character of the Russians. She loved them, but she wanted to make them over. Her mind was full of Voltaire and the philosophic reformers of the "Age of Reason." And deep in her heart was the freedom-loving idealism of her father. The ambitious young Queen had a dream of an ideal state.

This was not to be a republic, nor any form of democracy as we know it now—but an absolute monarchy. Only a strong ruler, thought Catherine, could save the Russian peasants from the vicious tyranny of their masters, the nobles. Under her kindly but dictatorial rule, government was to be efficient, small business and industry were to be encouraged, justice was to be fair, and the poorest were to be educated—and above all everyone was to be free. Every man and woman, thought the idealistic Queen, should be equal to everyone else.

There were a few other rulers in Europe in Catherine's time who were saying the same thing. "Benevolent despots," they were called. In truth they were only a short distance from modern democracy. Most of the world still believed that kings and queens ruled by Divine Right given them by God, and that they could do just as they pleased. But these new young kings and queens believed that they had a duty to their people, even to the very lowest.

What they could not see was that when their subjects had gained freedom and education they would want to run things themselves, without kings or queens, benevolent or otherwise.

But many of these level-headed rulers, including Catherine, unknowingly helped the world along the road to democracy.

Russia was still far behind the rest of Europe. Only seventy years before Catherine became empress, it had still been a barbaric, semi-oriental country. Women were not considered "souls"—a nobleman, in counting his serfs, listed only the men. Girls of the upper classes were kept under lock and key and never saw their husbands until the wedding day. After their marriage they never under any circumstances appeared in public, but were kept in a separate part of the house, like an oriental harem.

Everyone in Russia was the vassal, or slave, of someone higher than he. The highest noblemen were the slaves of the emperor, who was at the peak of the pyramid. They even called themselves slaves when speaking to him. Serfs were the lowest vassals, the peasant class. They depended on their lord for protection; and he, in turn, could order them to do as he pleased. Most of the noblemen, or boyars, lived comfortably and lazily in big country houses surrounded by their own villages. Their serfs worked the land for them in the most primitive fashion. There was no industry at all. Russia was a country rich in mines, but no one had ever bothered to work them. They hardly knew the meaning of coal and iron.

In religion, too, Russia was living in the Dark Ages. The Russians had not been Christianized until the eleventh century. Before that they had had a pagan system of high gods, demi-gods, nymphs and fauns almost exactly like those of the ancient Greeks—even many of the names were the same. When the first Christians came to Russia, the people allowed themselves to be converted with suspicious ease. Actually they took their gods with them into Christianity, and carried out the ancient rites in Christian churches. As time went on, the power of the old gods faded. But on holidays the peasants still observed the earthy, pagan rites which probably went back to Greek mythology. The prayers to the gods survived—and still do today—in the form of folk songs.

Peter the Great, who came to the throne in 1689, noted the high state of civilization in Europe, and determined to modernize his pagan, barbaric people. Ruthlessly energetic, he accomplished a miracle—but only in the thin top layer of Russian society. He fined boyars who persisted in wearing the national costume, a long, flowing oriental robe. His soldiers cut off the boyars' long beards in the streets. He ordered the women out of seclusion and sent soldiers to escort them forcibly to balls and operas, with threats of imprisonment for disobedience. He imported French tutors for the sons of the nobility and Germans to teach in the schools—although the few boys who went to school had to be driven there with whips at first. He forced the working of mines by declaring that an unopened mine could be worked by anyone who chose, without permission from its owner.

Under his headstrong tyranny the wealthy boyars and merchants became Europeanized and developed a vast snobbism for everything Russian. Everyone who could talked French, and merchants could always get three times the price for an article if they said it was made in England or Germany.

But the thin veneer of culture only gave the nobility a love of pleasure and luxury. With Peter the Great's reforms and his improvement of agriculture, industry and mining, the noble class became immensely wealthy. Under the feudal system boyars had owned serfs as a reward for having to serve the state. Now they no longer had to serve the state. They had nothing to do but gamble, dress beautifully, go to balls and grow richer and richer.

But they still owned serfs. In his reforms Peter had entirely neglected the lowest class. In fact he had used the serfs to build up the wealth and power of his country. Serfs were given to capitalists to work mines and run factories. Serfs were the forced labor that built the beautiful new city of St. Petersburg and the immense country palaces. Serfs built the canals and highways that carried Russia's produce to the cities. Serfs paid the taxes; the nobility was entirely free of taxes. And serfs were the main recruits for the army and navy. The entire glory of the new Russia rested on the backs of the laboring peasant class, who were given nothing in return.

Between Peter the Great, who died in 1725, and Catherine, who came to the throne thirty-seven years later, Russia had a succession of weak rulers. They depended for their thrones on the friendliness and support of the powerful feudal nobility. By the time Catherine came, the real rulers of Russia were the boyars and not the monarch. They were far richer than the aristocracy in Europe. They wielded absolute power in their villages, their vast estates and in the Senate, which was Russia's chief governing body.

And the last remnant of freedom had been taken from the serfs when, in the middle of the eighteenth century a law was passed forbidding them to move from one estate to another. They were slaves.

Russia sometimes seemed to the young Queen like a vast, sticky swampland into which her attempted re-forms would sink like stones. On one hand was the traditional, absolute power of the nobility, on which she, as a usurper and foreigner, must depend. On the other was the dense ignorance of the masses, which knew no other condition than slavery.

But Catherine was hopeful and ambitious because the Russian people, from rich to poor, were good material to work with. The Empress always felt re-freshed when she saw the extraordinary harmony and richness of Russian life. This was due to the national character—hospitable, adaptable, quick-witted, easy-going and of an enchanting gaiety.

The very language was warm, rich and musical. Some said it was akin to ancient Greek, the language of poetry. Most Russians had a natural gift for music. They sang constantly—soldiers sang while marching, countrymen sang in the fields, drinkers sang in the taverns. Two people talking would suddenly burst into melody and speak in a kind of musical dialogue.

In the country on still summer nights, the air vibrated with the songs of the surrounding villages.

The Russian people were friendly, polite and unendingly hospitable. When two Russians met, they took off their caps, bowed very low, shook hands, wiped their beards, kissed and called one another brother or father. A traveler could rest without fear in a robbers' den. A peasant would share his last crust of bread with a stranger. A nobleman usually had twenty or more to dine with him—uninvited guests who had simply called to find if the gentleman would dine at home.

For the most part the people were healthy and extraordinarily long-lived—many lived to be over a hundred. Robust and red-faced and inclined to be fat in middle age, they did not look like ill-treated slaves. There were few beggars, and one seldom saw a deformed person or one who stuttered or squinted.

The reason for their strength and glowing good health was that there were not enough people in Russia to exhaust its immense fertility. Even the poorest could eat well with little effort. The woods were full of birds and animals, the rivers full of fish. Although agriculture was at a very primitive level the fields yielded incredibly. In the north wheat was planted, sprang up and was harvested—all within six weeks. In the south and west were vast fields of rich black loam stretching as far as one could see and fantastically productive.

The peasants loved food, and they ate like lords. Fish was salted, smoked or made into a delicious cold soup with herbs and *kvass*, the Russian beer. This was considered a delicacy even by the nobility. Every peasant wife knew how to make caviar. They collected and dried wild mushrooms; they pickled cucumbers, cabbages, onions and radishes. They preserved pork and beef by smoking or salting, so they could eat meat all year round. Every family made its own bread and its own beer, the staples of the peasant diet.

Fruits, vegetables and meats were plentiful even in winter. Every spring an army of gardeners came from the country to Moscow and St. Petersburg to grow vegetables. Each mansion had a cellar room filled with ice, where these vegetables were carefully preserved. In the fall the peasants took their animals—pigs, cattle, sheep and fowl—to the nearest city. Sometimes they had to journey as much as a thousand miles, traveling five hours and resting five, day and night. In the city the animals were slaughtered and taken to a great open food market. There one saw huge piles of birds with their feathers still on; fish with heads, tails and fins; whole oxen and pigs. When bought, the meat was cut, frozen and put in the ice-filled cellars.

Even the poorest peasants were scrupulously clean. Their one-room huts, where chickens picked at the straw of the mattresses and baby pigs slept with the children, were scrubbed, polished and aired daily. Everyone went often to the public baths. In the hot, vaporous atmosphere of the steam room they washed with soap and bundles of birch twigs. Then they rinsed themselves by rolling in the snow outside, eighty or ninety degrees below the temperature of the bath.

Although their only tools were knives and axes, they were extremely clever at making things. All their houses, boats and furniture, down to the wooden bowls and spoons, were beautifully fashioned with these crude implements. As quick with their minds as with their hands, their shrewdness and cunning were legendary. No European could outwit a Russian, whether peasant or merchant. But they were interminably slow about every undertaking. They loved to talk and talk about what they were going to do. Whether they ever did it and whether it succeeded was a matter of mere chance. This caused intense irritation to Europeans who had any business with them. The Empress herself, efficient and speedy, was often exasperated to the depths of her orderly German soul by the Russians' relaxed attitude of timeless indifference.

Their only vices were drinking and stealing. Both were indulged in by all classes, from the lowest to the highest. Their drunkenness was usually gay and their stealing unremorseful. Pockets were picked even in the royal court. The King of Sweden, on a visit to St. Petersburg, invited some high Russian officers to dine with him. One of them stole a silver plate off the tables. No sense of guilt followed discovery. The thief would simply return the stolen article, if he were caught, and say with a grin, "I have done wrong, sir." Their drunkenness, though excessive, seldom led to fights. Two drunken arguers would approach each other with raised fists, shouting rich obscenities. When they came close, they would suddenly break into laughter and go off for another drink, arm in arm.

There was no malignance in them. They cared nothing for revenge, murder was almost unknown, and there was no religious or political fanaticism. Never in Russia had there been the religious wars, massacres and persecutions that plagued the other countries of Europe. With this tolerance went a natural spirit of democracy which cheered the optimistic young Empress.

This mass of easy-going, talented, attractive, ignorant, inefficient people Catherine set out to mold into her dream-form of the perfect state. She was full of energy and good will. But she soon found that reforming Russia was like trying to drink the ocean.

In the first place Russia was an enormous, sprawling country with few roads. Communications were so bad that half the land could be destroyed and the other half know nothing about it. Many of Catherine's orders never even reached the provinces for which they were destined. Other reforms went through a series of ignorant provincial officials and self-important petty noblemen, and often did not get beyond the outer edges of the two capitals, Moscow and St. Petersburg.

In the second place every attempted reform met with a black wall of superstitious ignorance.

In the third place the power of the nobility was so firmly entrenched that only a mass revolution would ever uproot it—and it rested entirely on the medieval, inhuman system of serfdom. The nobles would fight to the death before they gave up their slaves, on whom rested all their wealth and power.

Catherine's liberal views were well known. Her people loved her. But her nobles hated and feared her. Early in her reign, in 1764, there was an attempted plot against her. A group of nobles decided to rescue and raise to the throne Ivan, the great-grand-nephew of Peter the Great. This young man had been emperor briefly at the age of ten months. Elizabeth, who usurped his throne, had wept sentimentally as she lifted the baby from his royal cradle, handed him to the guards and consigned him to life-long imprisonment.

She had given orders that the baby Prince should be killed instantly by his guards if anyone tried to free him.

Prince Ivan was now twenty-four years old, and he had never seen the light of day. Catherine knew of the unhappy young prisoner and held no malice against him. In fact she had once gone to his dark dungeon and talked to him, trying to get him to become a monk. In that way she could free a miserable prisoner, yet he would still be no threat to her throne. Prince Ivan refused, his mind unhinged by his long solitude. Elizabeth's death order was never rescinded. His rescuers, the noble plotters against her throne, were at the door of his dungeon when his guards killed him.

This attempt made Catherine realize the formidable opposition of the nobles, and she decided to move slowly. Her first acts were sensible reforms with which no one could quarrel. She standardized the currency, reformed taxes, enlarged the salaries of provincial officials to prevent bribe-taking, abolished the huge business monopolies and gave privileges to small merchants.

Wishing to have a census of the population taken, she asked the Senate for a list of the cities and provinces of the empire. The senators did not even know how many there were, much less their names and locations. The efficient Queen sent five rubles over to the Academy of Sciences on the other side of the Neva and bought an atlas. This she presented to the Senators, and told them sternly to learn the geography of their country.

Aghast at the ignorance of the provincial governors, she tried personally to teach them their own business.

One governor had twenty lessons in one month from his sovereign. He went home chastened, much wiser —and bursting with enthusiasm for his learned and charming teacher.

The serfs who worked in the mines and factories were near revolt when Catherine came to the throne. These people were the most miserable in Russia. Their conscienceless owners worked them to death and paid them irregularly or not at all. The Empress ordered them to be paid and tried to ease working conditions. She sent soldiers to carry out her orders.

Free schools and hospitals were established for the poor, and doctors sent to country districts at the Crown's expense. Catherine gave 200,000 volumes to libraries, sent talented students to Europe to study, pensioned learned men and gave large money grants to academies of science and art.

New highways and canals were built and old ones improved. Many new towns were founded. St. Petersburg was almost entirely rebuilt under Catherine's direction. In the first year of her reign, she sat by a window in the palace and helplessly watched a fire which burned down 240 houses. Within three years she had them rebuilt of brick. Whenever there was a fire, Catherine gave orders that new houses were to be built of brick or stone, never of wood. During her reign the city blossomed as one of the most beautiful and cultured capitals of the world. She was called the second founder of St. Petersburg.

Although the young Empress was praised on all sides for her tactful kindness and her reforming zeal, all was not brightness in her personal life. There was a dark blot which she tried to hide from others, even from herself. But it was there, and it grew with the years—her dislike of her son Paul and his growing hatred of her.

Catherine got him the best tutors and tried to substitute good sense for the love of a mother. But she could never feel that he was truly her son. During his childhood, when tenderness between mother and son would have grown naturally, she was not allowed to see him. By the time he was hers again, his character was fatally warped and utterly alien to hers. From a frightened child he was growing into a fearful man, afraid of being poisoned, afraid of being murdered, afraid of being disinherited. With the years he became fanatically superstitious and dangerously moody and cruel. He worshiped the memory of his father, whom he had hardly known, idolized Frederick II of Prussia, detested everything Russian and fiercely condemned his gay, smiling mother. The two reacted against each other like highly explosive chemicals. To everyone else Catherine was charming and tactful. With Paul she was short, stern, always unpleasant. In her presence he could only stutter and glower. She would not allow him to take any part in government—in fact he never showed any desire to do so.

But he was her heir. She dared not disinherit him for fear of alienating still further the powerful aristocracy. Paul was not popular with them either. But if she deprived him of his blood right to the throne, they would have an excuse to rise against her.

When he was twenty-one this cringing, sickly young man, undersized, already balding, was married to a German princess. Catherine chose her son's bride, and she chose well. Marie—a big, healthy, placid blonde girl—was good for Paul. Neither of them liked Catherine's court. They could not keep up with the sparkling company, and they were quite aware they were not wanted. They retired to a country palace far from the capital. There Marie, domestic and complacent, tended her flower gardens; and Paul trained his German soldiers. For a few years they were quietly content. Knowing her son to be in safe hands and far away, Catherine banished him successfully from her thoughts.

On another side, too, Catherine's personal life was not easy. She wanted neither husband nor children. Her experience with both had been too cruel. Eighteen years of marriage and life in the slippery, decadent court of Russia had taught her that she could depend on no one except herself. During those long years of fear and loneliness, she had learned to fend for herself, to take only her own advice. Strong-minded to begin with, the young Queen, by the time she reached the throne, was completely her own mistress, firm, even dictatorial. She was determined that no man should have power over her.

But she was still young and beautiful and vivacious, and she could not dominate her own heart—that heart which had always been eager for affection and quick to love.

The Orlovs, as the leaders of the revolution, were the most important dignitaries at Catherine's new court. The Empress gratefully showered them with gifts and titles. But smiling and relentless she refused to give any of the five brothers, even her favorite,

Gregory, a position of real responsibility. Desperately anxious to become emperor, he courted the Queen incessantly. But Catherine, though she looked on him with affection, gave him no encouragement. She had had a foolish husband for too long. Gregory Orlov, though handsome and brave, was not a man of outstanding talents.

But she remembered the sullen and gallant young lieutenant, Gregory Potemkin, who had torn the plume out of his hat on the day of her bloodless revolution. She sent for him, rewarded him for his part in the coup, and gave him a place at court. His defiant gallantry had attracted her then, and now she was delighted and surprised by his complex personality. Sometimes he was despondent and silent, at other times brilliantly witty. A ventriloquist and mimic, he could imitate Catherine's own voice perfectly and send her into peals of laughter. When she asked his advice on political matters, he was serious and unexpectedly astute. Deeply romantic at heart, he wrote sad love poems to his beautiful black-haired Queen and enchanted her with his open adoration.

Catherine saw that in every way his mind and his personality were superior to the very ordinary accomplishments of Gregory Orlov. Here at last was a man —and a young, handsome, entertaining man—who was truly her equal. But she was reserved. She did not want to offend anyone, or to give Potemkin any rash encouragement. As always, she was mistress of her emotions. And she had absolutely no intention of marrying.

Gregory Orlov, suffering from his futile dream of winning the crown, confided to his brothers his anger

at the love songs, the wit and the bold courting of
this young upstart. They fell on Potemkin one day, all
five of them, beat him up severely and put out one
of his eyes.

Potemkin appeared at court as usual the next day,
as bold, as witty as ever, a black patch over one eye,
his tall, soldierly figure erect. Catherine saw with
horror the patch, the blood, the bruises. Potemkin
never told her what had happened. But the Orlov
brothers had accomplished a result they never intended—the Queen was now openly and warmly sympathetic to their enemy. But soon afterward Potemkin
was sent to war, and Catherine sorrowed.

Then, in 1771, a plague of smallpox broke out in
Moscow. Every year countless people were killed or
disfigured by this terrible scourge. Vaccination was
known, but most people were afraid of it. Catherine
learned that it had been successful in curbing the
dread disease in England, and she wanted to free her
people, too, from this ever-present menace. As an example she decided to have herself vaccinated. Her
court was horrified. Everyone prophesied the immediate and terrible death of their Queen. But Catherine
had never put any stock in foolish terrors. She had her
doctor vaccinate her—and appeared at supper just as
usual. Within a short time several thousand nobles,
convinced, had followed her example.

But Catherine could not get the common people
to accept vaccination. It was considered a matter of
course that everyone would have smallpox sooner or
later. No one would think of calling a doctor for it.
When the epidemic broke out in Moscow, the sick
flocked to their wonder-working wooden virgins, where

the disease was spread. At every shrine there were praying crowds of dying people. Bodies lay in the streets, and the people rioted in their desperate attempts to get into the churches.

The Archbishop of Moscow, an enlightened man, thought that he might stop the riots and prevent the spread of the disease by removing the holy figure that was supposed to be the most effective. He had it secretly carried away at night. But the theft was discovered, and an angry mob went to besiege the bishop. He hid in the cellar of his own house. There the crowd found him and tore him limb from limb.

The plague was entirely out of hand. The soldiers could do nothing—indeed they were as panicky as the citizens. Catherine looked around at her court. Potemkin, fearless and devoted, would have been the man to help her. But he was far away in the south, fighting the Turks. Her eye lit on Gregory Orlov, moping over the failure of his hopes. Catherine, who hated to see anyone unhappy, gave him a chance to distinguish himself. She sent him out to calm the desperate, frightened crowds. He had been vaccinated, and went among the people without fear, persuading them to go home, calling doctors, seeing that the sick were isolated and arranging for the bodies to be removed.

In a short time the plague was under control, and Catherine built a triumphal arch to honor Gregory Orlov, the savior of Moscow. It was the only deed of consequence that this ambitious man ever accomplished. Catherine again looked on him with favor. But she did not forget Potemkin.

Three years after she came to the throne, the Empress turned her attention to law and justice. Russian laws were a mass of contradictions, and a judge could decide whatever he pleased. Lawyers had no special training. Their chief service was to tell the clients the best way of gaining the good will of the judge—this was usually a matter of some rubles passed under the table. The most popular and renowned lawyer in St. Petersburg had been a shopkeeper who could neither read nor write. He had been involved in so many law suits that he went bankrupt. But during these suits he had learned so much about the corrupt ways of judges that he made an excellent living as a lawyer.

Punishment was primitive and cruel. A woman who killed her husband was buried up to her neck in the ground and left there until she died. Pirates on the Volga River were hanged by the ribs from iron hooks and set adrift in a barge. Forgers had melted metal poured down their throats. Debtors were made slaves of their creditors. Torture was used as a matter of course; all court sessions were secret; a man could be imprisoned for many years without being brought to trial.

Catherine realized that to reform this monstrous, rotten system of justice would be the work of many years. But she determined to make a start. She would write an instruction, which lawmakers and judges could follow, and which would guide them gradually toward an ideal law system. For two years she closeted herself in her room for several hours each day, reading, studying and writing her fluent words.

She came up with a remarkable document—a blueprint for a perfect eighteenth-century state, with a

benevolent dictator at its head and full justice and
equality for all.

There were to be no torture, no arrest without
trial and no secret court sessions. Punishments were
to be mild, but must be carried out to the letter, re-
gardless of the class or wealth of the criminal. Everyone was to have equal right of trial, with a lawyer
assigned to defend him.

She provided in her instruction for an absolute monarch, who would curb the unfair power of the nobility
and enforce political and civil liberties for all the
people. Every person in the country, she wrote, had
a natural right to food and clothing, and no man might
be the slave of another.

It was a sane, liberal and philosophical document.
But in eighteenth-century Europe, where in most
countries the down-trodden masses were not considered
to have souls, Catherine's law instruction was looked
upon as revolutionary. In France, the country of her
spiritual teacher Voltaire, her document was forbidden
to be read.

And Catherine's own backward country was no-
where near ready for her progressive ideas. Democratic
the Russians might be by nature. But equality by law
for all persons—it was unthinkable!

In 1767, five years after she had come to the throne,
Catherine called a deputation from all over the country to present her law instruction. The deputies sat
for seventeen months, discussing, wrangling, cutting,
amending. At the end they had cut out about a third
of her work—and particularly every reference to free-
ing the peasants. Catherine realized that on this point,
to her the most important of all, she could never win

without losing her throne. But she lashed out bitterly at the noblemen who sat in the law parliament, regarding their angry Queen in stony silence:

"Of those who belong by birth to the unhappy serf class, who cannot break their fetters without committing a crime, one dares not say that they are just as good as we are. If even *I* say that I run the risk of being stoned for it. What do I not have to suffer from blind and harsh opinion when you, the noble mob, suspects that these discussions might bring some improvement in the present situation of the peasants? You defend with fury and passion the institution of serfdom, which in your innermost hearts you are obliged to condemn! I believe there are not more than twenty people in this country who will reflect sanely on the subject like real human beings. In fact I believe hardly anyone in Russia has ever entertained the thought that there could be any other condition for the peasant classes but that of serfdom!"

But Catherine's law parliament did not fail utterly. Many of her fair and just provisions were kept, and a beginning was made toward an equable law system. If the Empress did not succeed entirely, it was because impartial justice was impossible in a country where there was such a vast gulf between owner and slave. But the down-trodden in Russia were given new hope by their Queen's devotion to freedom.

Ironically, it was this new hope that led to the only serious uprising of Catherine's reign. When ten years had passed and the condition of the serfs was no better, they began to grumble. The Empress had given them the idea that they need not be slaves. And, since no

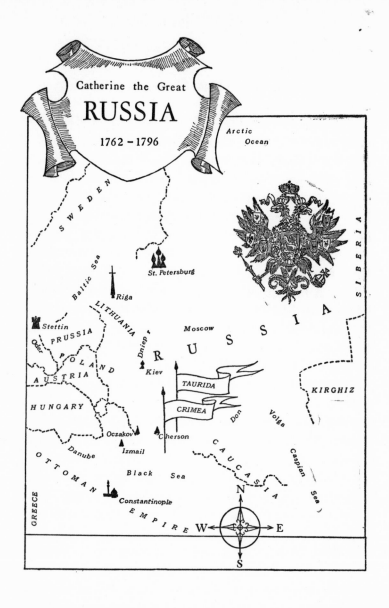

Catherine the Great
RUSSIA
1762 – 1796

Arctic Ocean

SWEDEN

Baltic Sea

St. Petersburg

Riga

LITHUANIA

Stettin

PRUSSIA

Oder

POLAND

AUSTRIA

HUNGARY

Dniep'

Kiev

Moscow

RUSSIA

SIBERIA

TAURIDA

CRIMEA

Don

Volga

KIRGHIZ

Caspian Sea

Oczakov

Izmail

Cherson

CAUCASIA

Danube

Black   Sea

OTTOMAN

GREECE

Constantinople

EMPIRE

N
W   E
S

one would do it for them, they were going to free themselves.

Their leader was a Don Cossack named Pugachev,
a homeless adventurer with blue-black hair, wild eyes
and a fiery tongue. He gathered resentful serfs around
him in the south, starting with the Cossacks, who had
always been a proud and independent people. But
Pugachev was a weak leader. He was not able to or-
ganize the rebellion into a serious revolution—particularly since he conducted it inappropriately in the name
of Peter III. Still, it raged sporadically for two years,
and had spread dangerously all over the southeast before it was quelled. In 1775, the year of the beginning
of the American Revolution, Pugachev was captured,
brought to Moscow in a cage and executed.

Russia was still a country of slavery. But the slaves
had seen the distant glimmer of freedom.

Most of Europe made fun of Catherine's reforms.
Seeing a few crumbling huts in a vast wasteland with
the name of a new city attached to them, or the decayed foundations of a new hospital, or a half-dug canal
abandoned and full of mud, Europeans called her reforming reign "a colossus of brass on a pedestal of
clay." Joseph II of Austria joked cruelly about it (although he was trying to do the same thing in his country). Catherine once invited him to place the second
stone of a town, of which she had already placed the
first. Joseph said privately to a friend later—and the
remark was quoted all over Europe:

"I have finished in a single day a very important
business with the Empress of Russia. She has laid
the first stone of a city and I have laid the last."

It is true that Catherine was over-ambitious for her country and tried to do more than was possible. But she accomplished far more with her friendly efficiency and high-hearted idealism than had the heavy-handed, cruel, half-mad Peter the Great. Greatly beloved by all her people, she led them with a gentle hand along the path of enlightenment. Her tools were tact, humaneness, shrewd knowledge of character and smiling, tireless energy.

If many of her projects had noble beginnings and mean endings, still more bore fruit later. Projected towns which in her day were only signposts in a swamp, grew to be important cities. Free hospitals and district doctors began to prevent the spread of plagues and infectious diseases. Free schools gave the poor people their first glimpse of education. Grants to talented students, learned men and academies were an incentive to learning. Her encouragement of science, literature and art was not appreciated during her reign. But it flowered later in the tremendous intellectual upsurge of the nineteenth century, when Russia was to be one of the world's leaders in literature, music and art.

Here and there she succeeded in abolishing serfdom, and she firmly prevented its spread into new territories. Catherine gave to the serfs themselves, if not to their masters, the realization that they did not have to be slaves.

Even in her own day it was said that Russia, a dark country, shone from the reflected glory of Catherine.

7 The Soldier-Monk

Catherine's chief interest in the early years of her reign was to make Russia a better and happier country. To do this she must at all cost avoid wars or trouble along the boundaries. Russia, being the most powerful nation in Europe, could easily stay out of war. But most of Europe in those days was ruled by touchy princes or kings who were given to starting wars at the slightest insult, or picking off little pieces of one another's land without asking leave. Russia had two dangerously weak boundaries where it would be easy for jealous or greedy monarchs to make trouble. One was the western edge where Poland lay, sick and weak, torn by internal dissension, a ready prey for any hungry European ruler. The other was in the south, where the ancient Ottoman (Turkish) Empire was also rotting from within. Here nomadic Tartars and wild Caucasian mountaineers constantly swooped down on the Russian villages precariously perched on its boundary.

These two boundaries had to be safeguarded. But the idea of safety grew with the years into the idea of expansion. Catherine remained a sane and kindly ruler in her own country. But her power was so great that it went to her head; she became a conqueror outside of Russia. And at last she found herself, as have most conquerors, in such an involvement of wars that Russia was very nearly ruined.

When Catherine came to the throne, the most immediate danger was Poland. Frederick II of Prussia, on its west side, and Maria Theresa, Empress of Austria, on the south, hovered over the sick country like vultures, ready to gobble it up. Catherine was determined to keep Poland whole. She wanted a safe, friendly Poland between Russia and those two, the most voracious monarchs in Europe.

As in her internal reforms, Catherine did not depend on anyone to do her work for her. She was her own foreign minister. Much as the other countries of Europe disliked and feared the tremendous power of rich Russia, they all had to admit that its ruler was a genius. An astute and wily diplomat, Catherine could wind foreign ambassadors around her fingers with gracious charm. Meanwhile, with a whispered word or a promise made in the right place, she reached behind them and quietly settled affairs to suit herself. In this manner she succeeded in influencing politics in other countries long before anyone there realized he had been influenced.

Poland had always chosen its kings by election. The nobility would gather in an open field and vote freely. In 1764, when an election came due, Catherine chose one of her admirers, Poniatovsky, who was of noble Polish blood. She made promises to the Polish nobles and bribed Frederick II, who liked money even more than power. Poniatovsky was elected King of Poland. To insure the outcome of the "free election," a large number of Russian troops had camped menacingly near the election field.

But Poland was still a danger spot. Stingy Frederick II was induced by Russian money to hold off for a while. But Maria Theresa, pious, hypocritical and predatory, could not be bought off. She disliked the thought that Russia was the most powerful nation in Europe. And she wanted to make trouble for Catherine, whom she hated personally. Catherine's sunny temper and easy gaiety indicated to the dour old lady a lack of morals. In 1770 Maria Theresa prayed and wept, and then she took a little piece of Poland. "My dear worthy Lady Prayerful," said Catherine, who hated Maria Theresa equally, "has taken a bite out of Poland. It seems that in this Poland one has only to stoop and help oneself."

Frederick followed the example of the Austrian Empress and took another little piece. And in 1772, to protect her own boundary, Catherine took some of eastern Poland. This had actually been part of Russia originally, and most of its population was Russian.

It happened twice more, and by 1795 there was no Poland left. A stern, hostile and unhappy deputation of Poles came to see Catherine and plead for their country. The Empress received them, radiating dignity and benevolence. After talking to them for a quarter of an hour she withdrew, making a slow, stately curtsy. The Poles, who had just lost their country, were captivated.

"No, she is no woman," said one of them. "She is a siren, a magician. It is impossible to resist her."

Although Catherine had the art of winning over her enemies, she was not happy at the destruction of Poland. It was not at all what she had intended. A friendly, secure Poland would have been a much greater advantage to Russia than these seething, unhappy provinces, over which two greedy and unscrupulous monarchs could stare directly at Russia's boundary.

Still, the partitions of Poland gave Russia many thousand square miles of fertile land, much of it already Russian in population. And Russia's boundary was now safely far from Moscow and the vulnerable Volga basin. Catherine, contemplating the ease and peacefulness of the partitions of Poland, became more than ever sure of her power. She began to be dangerously fond of conquest.

The great Ottoman Empire, which had lasted longer than any empire in history, was now rotten to the core and ready to fall apart. The Sultan had no control over the outer edges of his vast lands, and wild hordes of Tartars roamed freely along the Russian borders, massacring and pillaging. Catherine realized that southern

Russia would never have peace until its boundaries were extended to the natural fortress of the Caucasus Mountains. She made cautious, diplomatic steps in this direction, anxious to avoid a war.

But Europe was fearful of the influence Russia was gaining under its astute and ambitious young Queen. Several monarchs got together and decided to make trouble for Catherine. In 1768 they goaded the Turks into declaring war on Russia. It was at this time that Potemkin, with a black patch over his eye, was sent to fight.

The Russian army won several brilliant victories and destroyed the Turkish fleet. But after this the war dragged on for several years without much happening. Catherine had hated it from the beginning. Now she knew that her soldiers were bored, sick and miserable in the disease-ridden swamps and forests where the Turks preferred to fight their guerilla warfare. She determined to put a stop to it.

Catherine was used to being her own minister of state. But this time she decided to send Gregory Orlov to make peace. He was still fuming bitterly over his failure to become emperor, and she wanted to take his mind off it by giving him another chance to be a hero. She gave him detailed instructions and sent him off to the south. But the young courtier, though courageous and attractive, had no skill in diplomacy. And at this time, ill from self-indulgence and too much high living, he was losing touch with reality. He swaggered around in a suit entirely covered with diamonds, which had cost a million rubles. He boasted of his high position at court, offended and insulted the Turks. Then suddenly, in the middle of the peace talks, he inexplicably went back to St. Petersburg and started giving lavish parties.

What was the matter with these Russians, wondered Catherine, who never allowed wealth and power to overcome her simple, frugal way of living. She received Gregory Orlov at court with smiling gentleness, looked closely at the wild eyes and the sick face, gave him a lot more rubles and sent him off to an estate in the country. Shortly afterwards Gregory Orlov died, insane, victim of his own lack of self-control.

Catherine knew one of whose diplomacy she was sure. That was Potemkin, still fighting in the sporadic southern war. She entrusted the peace talks to him. Within a few months he had made a highly advantageous treaty. Russia got the province of Azov, which gave her control of the shores of the Sea of Azov. She got the Straits of Kerch, which united the Azov with the Black Sea. And she got the mouths of two great rivers that emptied into the Black Sea, the Bug and the Dnieper. Even more important, the wild Tartar clans of the Crimea were made independent of the Sultan. They were not yet subject to Russia. But the way was open for the Russians to civilize and tame them, and so make the southern boundary safe.

This treaty was the beginning of a grandiose and fatal dream. The Turks owned the Black Sea and the Sea of Azov, and prevented Russian produce from reaching Europe by ship in the south. Catherine envisaged a time when the shores of these seas would be entirely Russian, and Byzantium and Greece too, and Russian ships could sail freely through their own inland seas, along the shores of their own Middle East, out into the Mediterranean. This dream held her for

thirty years of her reign. It has held every Russian
ruler since her time. And it still has not come true.

But Catherine saw the beginning of her dream
come true in Potemkin's treaty. In Moscow she ex-
ulted and praised the young statesman. "Ah! What a
good head the man has," she said. "He has had the
greatest share in this peace. And this sound head of
his is amusing as the devil."

Potemkin came back to Moscow, but he did not join
in the celebrations. Although his Queen had praised
him, he did not think that she loved him. For years she
had, with smiling tact, steadfastly frustrated the hopes
of Gregory Orlov. Might she not do the same with
Potemkin—heap him with wealth and titles and keep
him near her as a kind of glorified court jester? The
keen young man knew that Russia would never have an
emperor while the strong-minded Catherine lived. But
he was too ambitious and too clever to be content with
the position of a court favorite. Besides he hated the
pomp and formality of court life. He was a soldier and
was at his happiest when he was in the field with his
men, living as they did.

He still loved Catherine as he had loved her when
she was a suffering bride. Now she was powerful and
successful and could do as she pleased, and Potemkin
felt himself no more than her servant. He fell into a
profound melancholy. At this time of his triumph,
when all Russia was grateful to him and his beloved
Queen honored him with her open-hearted praise and
affection, he suddenly retired to a monastery and declared his intention of becoming a monk.

"An unfortunate and violent passion," he wrote
to a friend at court, "has reduced me to despair. In

this sad situation I thought only to fly the object which causes my torment, since its sight could but aggravate my sufferings, which are already intolerable."

This letter was repeated to Catherine. She had admired Potemkin's wisdom and diplomacy in dealing with the Turks. She had liked his boldness, his wit and his poetic adoration. Not temperamental herself, she was now surprised and upset by his unhappiness. The one-eyed giant had won her heart.

"I cannot understand," she said to Leo Narishkin, always her friend and confidant, "what can have reduced him to such despair, since I never declared against him. I fancied, on the contrary, that my friendliness must have assured him that his homage was not displeasing. He will come back soon."

But now Catherine learned something of Potemkin's character that he had never spoken of to her. His retirement was not due to a passing mood. It was rooted in a profound mysticism. He had never lost his longing for the exalted solitude that the life of a monk offered. It was not only melancholy that sent him to the monastery; it was the deep faith of the medieval man. Catherine was aghast when she learned of her courtier's true intention. Much as she loved the Russians, the rational and practical German princess could never understand their unreasoning mystic faith. Sorrowing, she saw that Potemkin was a child of his people, a true Russian. Was she to lose him because of this? He stayed away month after month, and Catherine wrote, pleaded, ordered.

He came back as suddenly as he had gone. Changeable, vivid, adventurous and ambitious, a natural leader, Potemkin had discovered in his months of quiet solitude that he was not cut out for the life of a recluse. And he could not stop loving Catherine. In his lonely retreat he, too, had suffered. Thirteen years after they had met, Potemkin and his Queen entered on the partnership which was to last until his death.

It was a strange attraction: the sane, literal, efficient German Princess, with her plain Lutheran background; and this mystical, moody, brilliantly erratic Russian, half soldier, half monk, a creature out of the eleventh century, and the very essence of Russia.

They had one similarity—they were passionately ambitious for their country. They loved each other, but they both loved Russia more.

Potemkin, Catherine soon found, was not an easy man. He never allowed himself to be under anyone's control—not even the Queen's. He was often rude; sometimes he would not even speak to her. He would shut himself in his bedroom for many days. There a servant would read poetry to him while he lay on a sofa, clad only in a dressing gown, and toyed with a handful of uncut jewels. He would appear at a court reception in the same dressing gown, munching on a raw turnip, his hair hanging uncombed about his ears. Hating the formalities of the court, he would chew his fingernails, fidget and suddenly leave the room. But nervous as he was in court, he could stand all day in church at a mass.

Sometimes, with an abrupt change of temper, he would dress in the most elaborate and expensive finery, cover himself with all the orders that had been bestowed on him until he looked like a ribbon-vendor at a fair, and display Catherine's diamond-studded portrait in the midst of them. He would send a courtier a hundred miles to fetch a nosegay and a bunch of grapes for his Queen and pay all her debts without telling her.

He became extremely wealthy. Bundles of banknotes were bound as books and ostentatiously displayed in his library. But he often forgot to pay his servants. Then, contrite, he would shower expensive gifts right and left with improvident generosity.

Though not a scholar, he had an excellent memory and the knack of gaining knowledge from others. What he did not know he had an uncanny talent for guessing. The most learned men were astounded by his apparently wide and profound knowledge. But even with learning he was capricious. His one eye twinkling, he would discuss religion with generals and military tactics with archbishops.

There was a magic in his personality which no one could resist—and a freakish perversity which often irritated those around him to the last end of exasperation.

The Queen often did not know what to do with this extraordinary, unpredictable genius she had lifted to the highest place in the state. But she was easy-going and tolerant of other people's moods. When he felt affable, he fascinated her with his wit and knowledge. And she continued to be enchanted by his romantic barbarousness, so alien to her down-to-earth personality. Even his rudeness and independence were attractive to her; she had always hated slavishness. When a courtier flattered her, she would turn to her little dog and say to it:

"Listen to me, Pani, you know that I always push you away when you cringe. I do not like servility."

This half-savage, medieval man Potemkin was unexpectedly wise in government. Catherine made him governor of the new Russian province of Azov, and he busied himself immediately in building towns and encouraging agriculture on the wild, fertile southern steppes. The new lands had been mostly given over to sheep and cattle. But Potemkin invited experienced farmers to emigrate from western Europe. They were promised homes and tools with which to start modern farming operations.

His main concern was to prevent the spread of serfdom to the new domain. There were no large landowners, and Potemkin organized groups of inhabitants along the hereditary communal lines of the proud and independent Cossacks. No man there was the slave of another, and all shared work and produce equally. Potemkin, like Catherine, intensely disliked the institution of serfdom; though he himself eventually owned thousands, tenants of the lands Catherine gave him.

The new governor spent months traveling among the Tartar camps in the Crimea assiduously winning over the wild chieftains. Again like his Queen he hated unnecessary war and bloodshed and determined to accomplish everything with peaceful means. By a mixture of bribes, threats and promises, many of the Tartar Khans were persuaded to place themselves under the protection of the Russian Empress. Still others resisted, but there was almost no fighting. The Tartar method of resistance was simply to pack up and leave. A trifling uneasiness or a little disgust would cause a Tartar tribe to fold its beehive-shaped tents, pack them on the backs of small, shaggy ponies and depart suddenly in the night. Used to living entirely on sheep and wild fruit, the tribe might travel idly for several months. And then, unexpectedly, it would return.

Potemkin had such success with the Tartars that in 1783 Catherine formally annexed the Crimea. She promised to respect the Tartars' ancient customs and give them absolute liberty in the practice of their Mohammedan religion. This promise was scrupulously observed.

With the same mixture of persuasion and promises, Potemkin gained for Catherine the ancient kingdom of Taurida, place of the earliest Greek legends. This southern kingdom, a cape jutting into the Black Sea, was a beautiful, dreaming land full of shade trees and fragrant flowers. Here the Tartars, wonderfully idle, lazily tended their sheep in the daytime and sat on their flat roofs in the long warm evenings, silently smoking their pipes. They could neither read nor write; and they did not entirely understand that now, instead of belonging to a distant Turkish Sultan, they would belong to an equally distant Russian Empress. They only knew that before this they had been happy. If they ceased to be so, they would quietly board the small ships they had built and sail down the Black Sea to Turkish Romania. But their ways were respected by the Russians, and they continued to lead their peaceful, lazy lives.

Potemkin was governor of Azov and the Crimea, and his sovereign now named him Prince of Taurida. He ruled an area larger than most European kingdoms. Most of it was rich flat land like our prairie country, where wheat could be grown and cities could be built. Potemkin made the beginnings of this development. Many criticized him because the cities did not spring up overnight, and money intended for their development was sometimes squandered by inefficient underlings. It was said that the foreign farmers did not find the tools and homes they had expected; that the army sent to protect the border was not regularly paid; that too many soldiers were withdrawn, so that some of the wilder Tartar tribes again started killing and pillaging. Many of these criticisms were just. But Potemkin, like Catherine, had to struggle with the vast ignorance and inefficiency that stood in the way of progress.

Unlike Catherine, he was hampered by the defects of his own personality. He was often indolent, often despairing, often extravagantly self-indulgent. He would bind his handkerchief, dipped in lavender water, around his forehead and retire for days, suffering from real or imagined headaches. Then he would suddenly emerge and give a party of Asiatic magnificence. Dressed in a coat edged with sable fur, with the diamond stars of his orders on his breast, he received his guests in a room with cloth of gold on the floor. In the center of the room was an enormous oriental divan with a cover embroidered in rose and silver, on which reclined ladies dressed like sultanas in many-colored gauzes. Arabian perfumes filled the air with cloying sweetness. Supper was served by tall cuirassiers with red capes, silver shoulder belts and high black fur caps. They marched in two by two, holding aloft flaming sticks on which were spiked steaks of tender lamb. Music was provided by a remarkable military band of fifty horns, each of which could play only one note. The musicians, all of whom had started as unlettered peasants, played with astonishing agility and precision.

Catherine knew all about Potemkin's parties, headaches, undisciplined extravagance and morose indolence. But she also knew that in spite of his excesses he had extraordinary ability as a statesman. Gradually, under his governorship, South Russia was becoming a civilized community. In 1787 the Empress decided to make a tour of her new dominions. Partly she wanted to see for herself what Potemkin had accomplished. Partly she wanted to cement the friendliness of her new subjects with her own warm and attractive personality.

This was the chance of Potemkin's life. All the extravagant wealth of imagination that his brilliant mind could command went to make this journey into a glamorous and glorious pageant. He wanted only to please his Queen, not to deceive her. They were partners in everything, and Potemkin knew that Catherine was perfectly informed of the exact state of affairs in the Crimea. But he also knew that she would adore the splendid pomp with which he would surround her. Even more important, he could impress the various European rulers and ambassadors who were invited to accompany the royal party.

In January, 1787, the party started from Moscow. Great bonfires burned beside the highway to light their way in the snowy winter twilight. They stopped at night in buildings which had been refurnished in the style of Catherine's Moscow palace. In places where there were no suitable buildings, Potemkin had had small, elegant wooden palaces built. These buildings had been made and decorated at great expense, and every luxury was provided for the royal entourage. But inevitably the Russian genius for inefficiency

showed itself. The palaces were draughty and uncomfortable. Usually there were bats in them, and the
company came to expect them. When a courtier once
jokingly came up behind a lady and put his hands
over her eyes, she screamed.

"Oh, it's probably just another bat," said one of
the other ladies off-handedly, without even looking
around.

They had sumptuous meals on gold plates, fresh table
linen at every meal and music to entertain them. But
the choirs were often out of tune, and the orchestras
played like bands at a street fair. One orchestra played
a single tune over and over, very loud. Catherine, who
did not like even good music, finally asked gently that
the orchestra cease playing.

"Oh, we can't do that," said the leader. "This is
Prince Potemkin's favorite tune." And Catherine smiled
graciously while the noisy music continued to offend
her ears.

In the Empress' carriage, which was decorated with
emblems of diamonds, foreign diplomats were alternately honored with her company. One of her courtiers would take gold coins from a large green sack and
shower them on the heads of the inhabitants, who
knelt as her carriage went by.

Crowds of people gathered on the way to see
the smiling Queen. There were dark-faced, slit-eyed
Lesghis in fur-trimmed, pointed red hats, who had
come from the border of China. Sons of the kings of
the Caucasus, giant mountaineers armed with bows
and arrows, rode on dazzling white horses almost covered with silver. Persian princes on dromedaries, their
sabers sparkling with precious jewels; archbishops in

rainbow-embroidered robes, their white beards coming down to their knees; Tartar nomads; English farmers; Arabian merchants—it seemed that all the world had come to see the Russian Empress on her triumphal tour.

So majestic and yet so friendly was she that her new subjects fell in love with her, one and all. Even the wild Tartars were charmed. On a steep hill one day the horses of Catherine's carriage started to run away. The Tartar villagers who had gathered to see their new Queen dashed in front of the galloping horses. Catherine, alone in her careening carriage, sat quiet and steadfast until the villagers had brought it finally to rest. Then she descended and offered them gracious thanks. And the Tartars, recently bandits and barbarians, cheered their courageous Empress with tears running down their cheeks.

Potemkin had troops visible everywhere in large numbers, in order to show Russia's strength to the foreign ambassadors. Particularly he wanted to impress the new Emperor of Austria, Joseph II. Catherine was trying to make an ally of this sharp-tongued young man, son of her late enemy, Maria Theresa. Austria sat menacingly on the west side of the decaying Ottoman Empire. If Catherine wanted to realize her plan for a sea outlet to the south, she had to be sure of the friendliness of that dangerous country.

She and Joseph II joked and boasted in their diamond-studded carriage.

"I have an army of at least 600,000 men," said Catherine, "from Kamchatka to Riga. And thirty millions of subjects, reckoning only the male population."

"My empire extends from the Swiss Alps to the lands of the Sultan," countered Joseph. "And at least eight different nationalities live happily together in it." He added smugly, "We are both better off than the unfortunate George of England, who has just lost half his American colonies."

Catherine laughed. "The English hang their heads to their stomachs since that deplorable adventure," she said. "I admire the courageous General Washington. But rather than sign the secession of the thirteen provinces as brother George has done, I should have shot myself."

They talked about restoring Greece, now owned by the Turks, as an independent nation. "But," said Joseph, "what in the deuce shall we do with Constantinople?"

"Constantinople is my affair," said Catherine, smiling secretly.

In this way they took many cities and provinces and countries, without any trouble at all, and light-heartedly divided up the Middle East between them.

When they weren't talking politics, they were having fun. Count Leo Narishkin, always a gay buffoon, had an enormous toy top, bigger than his head. This he spun for their amusement, until one day it buzzed and leaped and suddenly burst into pieces with a terrible whistling. Several bystanders were wounded and one of them had to be bled twice.

But in spite of the fairy-tale extravagance and the light-minded gaiety, Catherine accomplished more on this six-month journey than a hundred wily diplomats could have done in years. Not only was she irresistibly charming, she was truly interested in her new lands.

Peasants danced and sang as the galleys passed.

At important towns they stayed one or two days. Here Catherine would speak to town officials, inquiring into the prosperity and resources of the city. She received the citizens with engaging friendliness and encouraged each one in his aims, however small. She walked through the streets and questioned the townspeople. The direct simplicity of her interest made her beloved by all who met her.

When the party reached Kiev, there were eighty elegant galleys waiting to convey them down the Dnieper River. It was the beginning of spring when they set out. The sky was clear; the river sparkled in the sunlight; and the shore was green and inviting. Many miles of shoreline were laid out like an English park. Beautiful buildings faced the river, and groups of peasants danced and sang as the galleys passed.

Potemkin showed Catherine more than was there, The peasants were moved in the night from one village to the next, to put on the same show the following day. The places that looked so inviting were often towns without streets, streets without houses and houses without roofs, doors or windows. Catherine saw many false fronts and colonnades with nothing behind them.

But she was not deceived. She knew that Potemkin could not have succeeded so quickly in converting these uncivilized provinces into happy scenes from an operetta. But she—and also her companion, sharp-eyed Joseph II—observed that there was growing prosperity behind the showy façade. New little industries were springing up. There was agriculture on the flat, fertile plains where there had been only a few sheep and cattle. Real villages had been built everywhere, with no false fronts. The Empress was more impressed with her minister's small beginnings than with his grand show.

But she adored the grand show. And she made the most of it to help her new provinces both materially, with gifts, and spiritually, with friendliness and encouragement. Every resting day was a holiday. Gifts of diamonds and gold were given; there were balls, fireworks and illuminations for miles around. The merchants gave splendid parties and Catherine, radiant and fascinating, pleased everyone.

At one town the King of Poland awaited them. The unfortunate Poniatovsky had come three months before and had spent three million rubles in gifts—all this in order to see Catherine for three hours. He wanted only to plead for his torn country with the powerful lady who had given him his throne. As they supped together on the silk-hung galley, the hills beyond the shore were illuminated with a lifelike representation of Vesuvius erupting.

But Poniatovsky got nothing out of Catherine. In truth there was no promise or comfort that she could give him. Poland had been doomed from the day that Maria Theresa had taken the first bite out of it. Hiding her uneasiness, Catherine was cheerful and evasive. When the King rose to leave, he could not find his hat. The Empress found it for him and light-heartedly put it on his head. He knelt before her.

"To cover my head twice—ah, Madame, that is burdening me with too much kindness and gratitude." With this sad little gallantry, he bowed himself out and went home empty-handed to his tattered country. With a sinking of her heart Catherine realized that power and conquest were not always pleasant. Momentarily afraid, she looked ahead to a future of bloody retaliation for her present successes. But the position of a conqueror had already turned her head; she was set on her course and could not change. And after all, it had so far been almost entirely bloodless.

The end of Catherine's Crimean journey was the city of Cherson, a newly prosperous port on the Black Sea. There was no deception in the bustling activity of this town. And here Potemkin reached the height of magnificence. A throne had been prepared for Catherine which cost 40,000 rubles. Quantities of merchandise had been brought from Moscow and Warsaw and was displayed in elegant shops. The town was jammed with Greeks, Tartars, French, Spanish, English, Poles and others who had gathered to pay homage to the Empress—or simply out of curiosity. Such was the crowd that a room for the night cost a thousand rubles. Potemkin ordered the gates to be moved farther out to accommodate all the people.

Potemkin had arranged to have three new Russian ships launched while Catherine was there—the beginning of the fleet which the Empress hoped would one day sail through the Mediterranean Sea to Europe. She watched the ceremony with Joseph II, who was by now thoroughly impressed and a little fearful. The two monarchs sat under a canopy ornamented with gauzes, laces and garlands of flowers which looked as if they had come from a Paris milliner's shop. This delicate finery was the work of Russian soldiers, recently rough, untutored peasants.

But these talented soldiers could fight, too, thought Joseph uneasily, glancing at the smiling but awesome Queen beside him. Catherine was enigmatic. Who could know what she would attempt next with her colossus of an empire behind her?

After the launching of the ships, Catherine joined her minister, the Prince of Taurida. Together they looked over the busy harbor of Cherson towards the city of Constantinople, invisible across the shining sea. Then Potemkin led his Queen through the streets of Cherson until they came to the eastern gate. Over it was an inscription in Greek:

This is the road to Byzantium.

They looked at each other and smiled without words. Together they had brought Russia to the highest point of glory it had ever achieved. Their country was the undisputed leader of Europe. It had grown in wealth and territory far beyond anything in European history. It was well on the way to gaining the coveted sea route to the Mediterranean. The splendid Empress and her brilliant, saturnine minister felt that their partnership was at the top of its power.

They reached beyond it, to an alluring and impossible dream—to revive the empire of Alexander the Great and crown Catherine in Constantinople as Empress of Byzantium.

This magnetic fantasy was to cost Catherine's country dearly. And it was to cost Potemkin his life.

8 The Grandmother

The great summer palace of Tsarskoe Selo was silent at five in the morning. In the long northern summer day the birds had already been singing for two hours, and the sun was high. But Russians liked to sleep late, even the servants. No one stirred in the dim marble corridors.

Only in the apartments of the Empress was there a sign of life. Catherine the Great, Autocrat of all the Russians, was laying a fire in her bedroom.

As she turned from the fire it could be seen, in spite of the flowing lines of her blue velvet dressing gown,

that at fifty the once willowy Queen was growing stout.
Her face, though pleasant, was set in lines of command; her long chin and firm jaw had become ac-
centuated. But her eyes sparkled alertly and her hair
was still thick and black and shining.

With erect and graceful dignity she moved to the
dressing table. Swiftly she twisted her hair into a loose
chignon and splashed ice water on her face, neck and
ears. She gave a quick look around the tidy little room,
whose walls were of dark blue lapis lazuli and its floors
a pattern of mahogany inlaid with mother-of-pearl.
Then she stepped out the French door onto the terrace.

A small green leather divan and a plain table stood
in the sunlight. Behind them was an elegant colon-
nade, its delicately fluted stone columns painted in
many colors. As Catherine sat at her work table, she
looked out on a tiny green lawn surrounded by fragrant flower borders. Beyond this stretched two beautiful gardens. On one side was a formal one laid out
in the French style, with winding paths, neat hedges
cut in fantastic shapes, and ancient lime trees. The
other was an English garden, a riot of flowers, in its
center a lake with white swans.

Catherine smiled happily at the freshness and fragrance of the morning and applied herself immediately to her work. She wrote almost without ceasing
for three hours with a quill pen in a large, free, flowing hand. She was writing a new play, a satire on the
sentimental and superstitious traits of human nature.
When she had finished, it would be produced as others
of hers had been since she had become queen. She
would be named again "The St. George of enlighten-

ment, striking down the dragon of superstition." The Empress remembered with a slight smile her earliest plays, written in the secrecy of her locked room at night, in fear that someone should find her at this shocking practice!

But she did not finish her play this morning. A thought struck her, and she flung aside the written sheets and pulled fresh paper to her. She would write a fairy tale for her two grandsons, Alexander and Constantine, four and three. They were the sons of her fearful and superstitious son Paul, of whose character she always made fun in her satirical comedies. At the thought of the beautiful and beloved grandchildren, so unlike their half-mad father, Catherine's firm face softened.

These two, Paul's first children, Catherine had taken as her own. She was afraid that under Paul's influence they might turn out to be little doubles of their father. Madness ran in the family of the czars, and Catherine was determined to protect her grandchildren. Alexander, born in 1777, had been named in honor of Catherine's dream of Byzantium and of reviving the ancient empire of Alexander the Great. "A name is a spirit and an influence that matters," she wrote to a friend. "It is a pity that fairies have gone out of fashion; they would give an infant all that one wishes. I should have made them beautiful presents, and I should have whispered in their ears: Give him spirit, my ladies, just a little bit of spirit, and experience will do all the rest."

Constantine, born a year later, had been named after the last Christian emperor at Constantinople. In a spirit of exalted hope, Catherine determined that the new child should be king of Greece.

The Empress wrote at the top of the paper, "The Journey of Chlore." Chlore would make a journey to reach the top of a mountain, where grew a red rose without a thorn. She would gather it after a thousand dangers and a thousand toils. When the tale was finished, Catherine would direct that a little garden be made at Tsarskoe Selo. There would be an artful small mountain, with tiny models of Chlore and her adventures on its sides, and a red rose at the top.

In an hour she had finished the fairy tale. She turned to her letters. The long correspondence with Voltaire was over, she reflected sadly. For fifteen years the witty old philosopher had flattered her, instructed her, made her laugh, knitted stockings for her and sold her watches, which he hoped "would not disorder the finances of her small household." She had replied to his letters with her own agile, philosophic wit. Now he was dead, and she mourned him—his gaiety even more than his wisdom.

But the Empress had many other correspondents with whom she exchanged long letters full of her graceful humor and her sharp comments on world affairs. There was the frenchified German, Friedrich Melchior Grimm, who entertained the more intellectual European royalty with his amusing letters. There was the Prince de Ligne, subtle, caustic courtier and soldier in the service of Joseph II. It was de Ligne who first called her Catherine the Great. Habitually, in his letters, he addressed her as "Monsieur." There was Frederick II, whose mind was as quick as ever, though

he was growing sour in old age, and as stingy as his father. There was Diderot, the free-thinking French philosopher. To him she once wrote: "You philosophers
are lucky men. You write on paper, and paper is patient. Unfortunate empress that I am, I write on the
susceptible skins of living beings." Oddly innocent
still, Catherine had not a glimmer that Diderot and
Voltaire and the others who amused her so, preachers
of the ideal state, would soon be honored as the true
fathers of an exceedingly bloody and terrible revolution.

And there was always Potemkin to write to, her
beloved minister, who could not stand court life for
more than a few weeks at a time, and who was away
from her more than he was with her.

Only a small part of Catherine's enormous correspondence was literary. This morning she was dealing
with affairs of state, both foreign and domestic. After
nearly twenty years of her reign, Catherine still had
not given up trying to rule Russia personally. She
wanted to have a hand in everything that went on in
her own country and in the foreign offices of other
kingdoms. She managed to keep the reins of foreign
policy tightly in her own hands. But within Russia,
much bigger and more unmanageable than it had been
when she came to power, the task of central government was hopeless. The serfs were as miserable as ever.
The nobles, on whom Catherine still depended for her
throne, were wealthy, arrogant and absolutely powerful. Catherine hated this state of affairs, but for her
own sake she had to keep peace with the nobles. She
continued trying to improve the quality of local govern-
ments, to stamp out bribery, to introduce real justice

into the courts. As she dealt with these matters, she frowned in concentration; and for once she looked stern.

But her face cleared when her maid appeared, about half-past eight, her eyes still red with sleep, muttering apologies and stumbling over the doorstep. "Pooh," said Catherine with a smile. "Stop muttering and mumbling, Natushka, and get me my coffee." The maid backed away and a few minutes later appeared with the coffee. An entire pound went into the five cups the Empress drank. This remarkable drink was Catherine's only breakfast.

After dressing she went to prayers in the chapel that lay at the other end of a series of long, gilded, mirrored galleries. The rooms that opened off this noble corridor were of marble and mosaic and rare woods. Some were beautiful; some were in atrociously bad taste. One had walls decorated entirely with paintings by Flemish, Dutch and Italian masters. But these paintings were not in frames—they served as wallpaper. Where a picture did not fit, the workmen had snipped off a corner or an entire side. Some were even upside down.

In the chapel Catherine knelt through the entire service, bowing her head as solemnly as the most devout peasant woman. She had never, since her conversion, been truly religious. But dutifully and thoroughly she observed its outward forms. In public she would even kneel on the ground at the entrance to the cathedral and scatter dust on her diamond crown. A Russian Empress had to appear as pious as the lowest of her subjects.

The rest of this morning she spent in her study receiving people and transacting state business. Among others she had a visit from the British ambassador, irate and shocked. England had implored Russia's help in putting down the revolt of the thirteen American colonies. But Catherine had been gleeful at the discomfiture of the King of England, George III, whom she considered an obstinate bore with no talent for foreign policy. Openly she applauded the success of the courageous American rebels. She foresaw the birth of a proud new republic built along the lines of Voltaire's ideal state. It should be easy. The Americans were educated, free-thinking and independent—nothing at all like her attractive but hopelessly ignorant countrymen.

When the demands from England became more insistent, Catherine had suddenly made a bold decision. Taking the lead in Europe she declared that Russia would be neutral in the war of the American colonies and would trade with neither nation. This was an unexpected and terrible blow to England. England had been profiting vastly from her trade with Russia. She had got such a monopoly that almost all of Russia's produce was carried in English ships. English merchants made huge fortunes and maintained grand palaces in St. Petersburg. In addition to this lucrative trade, England badly needed the goods that came out of Russia: hemp, tar, grain, linen and—above all—lumber from Russia's vast forests and iron from her rich mines. Catherine's declaration of neutrality was a clear challenge to England's power on the seas as well as being an insult.

That day the English ambassador confronted Catherine with what he considered her perfidy. Was she not grateful to the king who had provided Russia with the means of getting her produce all over the world? Catherine answered that Russian ships could carry Russian goods as safely as English; that the Russians might not be born sailors, but you can train a Russian to do anything. As for the American war, she said: "Your parliament should gnaw their fingers, after the fashion of Prince Potemkin. That sets the blood in circulation. If their circulation remains calm now, after the deplorable adventures in America, I will call them plodding nags."

The Empress was in a good humor, and the angry ambassador could get nothing out of her except jokes. He retired, defeated. But Catherine's humor changed when she read the reports of the Russian ambassadors at the French and German courts on the conduct of her son Paul. Catherine had sent Paul and his wife, Marie, on a tour of Europe, hoping it would cure him of his dangerous depressions. Paul's mind had begun to deteriorate a few years after his marriage. In his youth he had been full of fears and obsessive superstitions. Now, to counteract his terror, he had developed a violent temper and indulged himself in vicious hatreds. He was obstinate, yet full of unpredictable caprices, and incapable of being faithful. "Only the one to whom I speak," he once said with sullen pride, "is an important personage in Russia. And that only during the time I speak to him."

In his distant country palace, surrounded by soldiers and protected like a fortress, Paul brooded silently over injustices. He often gave way to moods of deep despair which were accompanied by terrible headaches. Coming out of these trancelike states he would eagerly watch the sadistic punishments that passed for discipline among the German-trained soldiers of his castle.

His wife kept house like a strict German *hausfrau*, dealt patiently and calmly with her morbid husband and bore child after child. The family hardly ever emerged to join Catherine's sophisticated court. Catherine was glad enough not to see them. They added nothing to its brilliance. At court Paul was sour and moody, Marie openly disapproving. But the Empress thought that her heir, whom she could hardly bring herself to think of as her son, should have a little experience of the world. She was used to ordering people around, and she had ordered Paul and Marie to Europe. Obediently they went.

In Berlin Frederick II, aging, gouty and cross, had exerted himself to be pleasant to the heir to the Russian throne. The old monarch, stingy as his father, had a new coat made for the reception, and the whole capital was talking about this unwonted extravagance. He received the Grand Duke with his old gracious manner, which had so charmed Catherine when she was a little girl, and poured flattery into the ears of the affection-starved young man. It had been planned to give the play *Hamlet* for Paul's entertainment. But at the last minute it was canceled. Frederick had suddenly thought of the deadly parallel between Paul and Shakespeare's hero. Now Berlin was full of whispers—the murdered father, the usurping mother, the brooding, indecisive son. Catherine frowned as she read this part of the report. Paul would love these whispered rumors. He wanted to be a Hamlet, wronged by his wicked mother. He would go into one of his black moods of hatred and despair and think about murder.

The report from Paris was equally typical of her dreadful son. He had been graciously received by Louis XVI and his lovely, laughing queen, Marie Antoinette. In their presence, amid a gay and glittering crowd of courtiers, the Grand Duke had suddenly blurted out:

"If my mother thought that I had but a dog belonging to me that loved me, tomorrow it would be flung into the Seine with a stone around its neck." He said these words with a fearful coolness, and his ugly face had no expression at all. The courtiers shrank back with horror, and there was dead silence.

Cold fear touched Catherine as she read the terrible words. What would happen to Russia if this man became emperor? What would happen to her beautiful little boys? She could not see the tragedy that lurked behind Paul's growing insanity—the long-ago tragedy of a sensitive, ugly, lonely child, unloved and rejected by his mother at the age when he most needed her. Catherine herself had been unloved then, and Paul reminded her of all the cruelties of her early years at the Russian court—the debauched Empress, the crazy drinking, the toy soldiers, the torturing of dogs and beating of servants.

Only, she reflected, her son was not imbecilic like his father. He was morbid, fierce and dangerous.

She banished her thoughts and returned to affairs of state. About one o'clock she went into her anteroom, where her ladies awaited her. She smiled and spoke to each one in turn. To one girl, who was too sulky to smile back, she gave a mock scolding: "Come, have you beaten your maid this morning? I am sure that is why you are looking so sulky. I got up at five, and ever since then have been deciding matters that will please some and displease many. But I have left all my worries behind in my study, and arrive here in the best temper in the world." Unwillingly the maiden smiled.

Dinner was at two o'clock. Those who wished to enjoy Catherine's wit and gaiety at the dinner table had to put up with her bad cooks. She did not much enjoy food, ate little and never seemed to notice how anything tasted. Today the roast pheasant was burned. Catherine made fun of the grimaces at the table and joked with the servant who came to apologize. Her guests drank wine, but Catherine took nothing except a few sips from a glass of currant juice which stood beside her plate. The conversation was lively. How different, Catherine thought, from the tedious, silent meals of Elizabeth's dull entourage, or Peter's wild drinking parties. The gay and sophisticated tone of Catherine's court had attracted visitors from all over the world. It was seldom that the charming Empress did not match wits at dinner with a learned scientist, a philosopher or a cultured diplomat.

Soon after dinner the Empress retired to her apartments. There she read and sewed during the afternoon. She was working on a remarkable garment which she had invented for her little grandsons. It was all in one piece, and the child could simply walk into it, arms and legs at the same time. In contrast to the complicated and uncomfortable satin breeches, tight velvet jacket, buttons, ribbons, laces and garters with which the eighteenth-century mother had to struggle in dressing her son, Catherine's single, buttonless garment was a stroke of genius. She herself never tired of boasting about it, just as she boasted constantly about her beloved grandsons.

Later in the afternoon she called the two little boys to her, and they walked in the garden together. They were accompanied by an extraordinarily vicious pet cat, who would bite, snarl and dig his claws into the hands of anyone who tried to pick him up. Catherine appeared to enjoy her pet and gave him a playful slap when he scratched her. She measured the courage of her friends by their success in withstanding the attacks of this cat.

The tall, stout Empress and the tiny, delicate boys fed the swans and talked about their day. Alexander was full of prattle. He showed his grandmother what he had done that day: he could already write, spell and draw. He told her that he had learned to mount a horse and shoulder a gun. He asked if there were people on the moon, and if he had been born there.

Catherine answered his questions with serious interest and talked to him about politics. The four-year-old, almost too prettily delicate, looked at her sweetly and intelligently as she expounded the liberal ideas she had first learned from her father when she was Alexander's age. Catherine's heart melted with love. He should be the next ruler of Russia instead of his miserable father, she thought, not for the first time.

His brother, Constantine, was still a baby, but already Catherine was worried about him. He was fiercely jealous of his beautiful and talented brother, and always wore a dark, sullen manner. He hated fresh air and annoyed Catherine by burying his nose in the blankets at night to shut out the air. His lively and active grandmother was also irritated by his dislike of physical exercise, his sulky bad temper and his lack of mental effort.

In truth she expected too much of such a small child. And she did not understand that even at this age Alexander was a dark shadow over his life, blotting out all hope and ambition.

He is to be king of Greece, thought the optimistic grandmother. That is a warm and lazy country. He can be outdoors and breathe the soft air, and will no longer need to hide his head in the blankets.

There seemed to Catherine no reason why her beloved grandsons should not turn out well. She had taken them from their fierce, melancholy father and their placid, stodgy mother. They were surrounded with love and attention and were provided with the best tutors. She had drawn up a set of instructions for their education. They were to have no scolding and were to be treated gently so that they should not learn to fear people. As soon as they could read, they were to have lessons in philosophy, science, history and languages. Her ideas of education were startlingly modern. In the eighteenth century most children had to drone Latin like parrots for eight hours a day, and were beaten if they so much as blinked an eye.

The two children had everything needed for a happy childhood. Most important, their grandmother gave them the true motherly tenderness that she had never been able to grant to her own son. Then why was Alexander already, at the age of four, deceitful and full of guile? And why was Constantine's baby temper so vicious, his manner so surly? As Catherine walked in the lovely summer garden with the little boys, the cold thought of Paul touched her again like a snake. She put it away, and her smiling face turned toward the loved children did not change expression.

But it was there, a stone in the bottom of her mind. The terrible, hidden tension between Catherine and her son was the poison that was corroding the characters of her grandsons. They could not help being aware of it, and their loyalties were divided. On the rare occasions when they were allowed to see their parents, Paul and Marie talked with bitter hatred of the woman who dominated their lives. Catherine herself never spoke to the little boys of their parents. But she was openly teaching Alexander how to be an emperor. Unknowingly she had already planted a seed in the little boy's mind. Very soon after her own death, this seed would blossom horribly into murder.

"Come, we must go in to tea," she said, suddenly cheerful, "and I will read you my new story of Chlore and the Rose Without a Thorn."

After tea Catherine went to prepare for a reception for foreign diplomats. Her hairdresser piled the wonderful hair high in an intricate arrangement of curls, pompadour and chignon. She chattered with him and joked with her maids as they dressed her. But when she stood up and slowly drew on her long white gloves she changed from an agreeable and facetious woman to a reserved, majestic empress. She seemed to grow taller, and her strong left hand held the fan as if it were a scepter. With slow, dignified grace she moved down the mirrored salons to the state drawing room.

"The Semiramis of the North," whispered one awed diplomat to another as they watched her queenly

The Empress walked in the garden with her grandsons.

progress, and thought of the immense, heavy power behind her, of the massive Russia she had made her own.

The reception over, she retired to her private drawing room with her friends. There again she shed her majesty, and the room became a scene of easy gaiety. Some of the younger courtiers danced. Catherine smiled at little Alexander, who was dancing with a giggling fourteen-year-old maid-in-waiting. A few of the older people sat down to play cards, and Catherine joined them. But she looked around the room constantly to see if everyone was at ease. Once she called a footman to draw the curtains because the late sun was shining in someone's eyes. She noticed an old gentleman who was not talking to anyone. Leaving the card game, the Empress sat with him for half an hour to make him feel part of the group.

Loving laughter, Catherine wanted only smiling faces around her. Although she no longer danced, she watched dancing with delight. She had even learned to like card-playing, but the Russian passion for gambling was forever mysterious to her. She had been known to discourse seriously for seven hours at a stretch with French philosophers. But her drawing room was usually a scene of youth, frolicsomeness and wit; and she was the center of it.

Only one thing she would not tolerate—that was scandal. The moral tone of her court was high. Sarcasm, gossip and intrigue were absolutely taboo. This, together with Catherine's own intellectual charm, gave her court a graciousness unknown in other European royal courts. The Russian Empress was better loved in the eighteenth century for her attractive court than she was for her conquests and her reforms.

At nine o'clock supper was served—another of Catherine's mediocre meals. This time she ate nothing, but walked among her guests, chatting and seeing that they were served. One lady held up her plate without looking, thinking that a lackey was behind her. The plate was taken by a smooth, long-fingered hand with an enormous solitaire diamond on one finger. The lady looked up, startled, and met the laughing, roguish eyes of her Empress.

One of the tables was mechanical. When the diner pulled a cord under the table, the plate sank down. Then he wrote on a slate what he wished to eat next and pulled the cord again. The slate disappeared, and soon the next plate arose with food on it. This toy delighted Catherine. The Semiramis of the North was not above childish pleasures.

The Empress retired at ten o'clock, and very soon afterward the rest of her company dispersed. By eleven the great palace was silent again. Outside in the quiet, flowery garden it was still blue twilight, and in the east one could already see the lighter glow of the coming sunrise.

9 End of the Dream

When Catherine had stood with Potemkin in 1787 at
the gate that led to Byzantium, she felt herself at the
top of her power. She was no longer young; but her
mind was as strong as ever, and her country was unchal-
lenged.

But the year that started with Catherine's triumphal journey through her new southern empire ended
on the bitter note of a new war. The Ottoman Empire
gathered its waning forces together, determined on a
desperate gamble to save itself from extinction. A

month after Catherine got home from the Crimea, the
Sultan declared war on Russia and Austria.

At first Catherine was happy with this news. It was
brought to her in the midst of a splendid ball at Tsarskoe Selo. She halted the dancing and had her herald
read the announcement. The elegant ladies and gentlemen cheered and clapped, and Catherine smiled
from her golden throne. She saw in this new war an
excuse to carry out her cherished project of taking
Constantinople and restoring the empire of Alexander.

Besides, she had won the friendship of Joseph II of
Austria. Between them they would make short work
of the Turks. Filled with high hope, she sent Potemkin off to the south to be commander in chief of the
allied armies.

The Russian army that confronted the Turks was at
that time the best in the world. It was generally admitted in Europe that the Russian soldiers were far
above all others in strength, courage, loyalty and skill.

Their training was brutally thorough. Only a Russian serf, accustomed to poverty and the rough life of
this half-civilized country, could have stood it. A peasant was taken from his wife and children by force and
made a soldier for the rest of his life. A wife was not
allowed to go with her soldier husband. Her noble
master quickly married her off to someone else so she
would not have to be supported by the nobleman.

When a new company of soldiers was formed, an officer lined them up before him. He pointed to them
one by one and said: "You shall be tailor to the company; you shall be shoemaker; you shall be musician;
you shall be cook." If they grumbled, they got a few

blows with a stick. They were continually beaten until they learned to make a shoe or play a fife. Adaptable and tough-minded, they learned their new trades with extraordinary quickness. In a short time the savage, timid peasants were transformed into neat, versatile, courageous soldiers. They could cook, sew, make shoes, build a house or play a musical instrument. Accustomed to rolling naked in the snow after coming from the heat of the steam bath, they could endure any kind of heat or cold. They could travel thirty miles a day with no more than a biscuit and an onion to eat. They sang and danced in the deep snow; they lay for many days in muddy trenches, joking under heavy cannonades.

An army of such brave and talented soldiers should have been able easily to beat the Turks. The soldiers of the Ottoman Empire were casual in war. They never fought at night and never got up early in the morning. No battle started before ten o'clock. On their many holidays they would not fight at all. They would wrap cannon balls in rags and lob them gently into the Russian camp, not intending to hurt anyone. In the meantime the Russian officers played checkers or gambled, drank wine and gave exotic parties.

When a battle was joined, the Turkish soldiers would scatter over the countryside, hiding in holes. They would suddenly leap out of their hiding places and advance with frightful howls, carrying heads on pikes. Backing up the guerilla foot soldiers the cavalry came shrieking toward the enemy, making their horses prance frighteningly. This exhausted the horses, but it had no effect on the stolid Russian soldiers. Unimpressed by howling Saracens and prancing horses, the

Russians calmly stood still and fired their guns. Usually the Turks fled in all directions.

When Turkish prisoners were brought in, the Russians laughed at them. With their wide silk pantaloons and their curved scimitars, they looked more like figures in a ragged masquerade than like soldiers. On Potemkin's orders prisoners were treated gently. Once four of them, captured by a band of Cossacks, were brought before the commander in chief. They cringed miserably, expecting to be killed. Potemkin glanced at them carelessly and ordered them to be thrown into a tub of water.

"Now you are blessed with a Christian baptism," he said, turning away.

It seemed a play war. But months and finally years dragged on, and the disorganized Turkish army was not beaten. A strange lethargy seemed to have overtaken the Russian generals. Catherine gradually came to see that this stemmed from Potemkin. Wise as a diplomat and governor, the soldier-monk turned out to be a weak leader in active war. Not only did he hate bloodshed, but he was oddly soft-hearted. He would hesitate for weeks or even months to give the order for an assault, fearing that many of his soldiers would die in the battle. He would weep when the Turks attacked and tremble at the sound of distant cannon.

Yet as a soldier in the field Potemkin was at his happiest. He had high courage and would stand unmoved, smiling and joking, as cannon balls fell around him. He could go for days eating only onions. He endured the fatigue, the mud and the primitive life as cheerfully as any of his soldiers. In open battle, leading his men, Potemkin was superb. All his soldiers adored him.

It was only in his tent, alone, with a decision of bloody battle to be made, that he hesitated, sick with worry and fear.

Joseph II, disturbed by the slowness of the fighting on the Russian front, sent his henchman, the Prince de Ligne, to watch Potemkin and report to him. Catherine made de Ligne a field marshal, and he spent most of his time trying to bully, bribe or taunt Potemkin into getting on with the war.

"I will have you named governor of Moldavia and Wallachia when we conquer them," said de Ligne, "if you will take this town of Oczakov." Oczakov was an important port on the Black Sea, before which Potemkin had been lingering for months. He was afraid to give the order to assault it and hoped to take the town by negotiation. The mud and heat were almost intolerable. Lizards and tarantulas crept into the tents at night, and the water was bad. Even the healthy Russian soldiers were sickening, and supplies were running low.

"What do I care for Moldavia and Wallachia," said Potemkin. "I might be king of Poland if I chose. I have already refused the duchy of Courland." He added disconsolately, "But this confounded place plagues me."

"It will plague you a long time yet," answered de Ligne, "if you do not proceed more vigorously."

"But we have no provisions. We are in need of everything," said Potemkin. "I have sent for things, but they do not arrive." He was in one of his dark moods of despondence.

De Ligne laughed. "Yes, if we had provisions, we should march. If we had pontoons, we should cross rivers. If we had balls and bombs, we should begin the siege. Nothing else has been forgotten." Potemkin smiled sourly and went back to his tent. He wrapped a wet handkerchief around his forehead, said that he had a headache and was not to be disturbed.

Catherine added her pleas to de Ligne's barbed taunts. "If you wish to roll a stone from my heart," she wrote to him, "if you wish to free me from a heavy nightmare, then begin operations at once by sea and by land. Otherwise you will drag out this war still longer. And that you can wish just as little as I."

But Potemkin still hesitated, alternating between lonely fits of despair in his tent and elaborate entertainments. At one of these parties a court lady appeared masquerading as a gypsy and pretended to tell his fortune. Potemkin, impatient and inattentive, gnawed at his fingernails while the lady spread out her cards.

"I predict that you will take Oczakov within three weeks," she said.

The one-eyed giant stood up and scattered the cards in sudden anger. "I have a method of divination far more infallible," he answered hotly. He left the party, called his generals to him and ordered the town to be attacked the next day.

Oczakov was taken by sea and by land. A year and a half after the start of the war the Russians had won their first victory. It was a terrible and bloody victory. At least 9,000 Turks died. The Russian soldiers had few losses, but thousands of them had died of disease before the town while Potemkin indulged his moods.

Oczakov was taken by sea and by land.

After this battle he was in high good humor. Catherine gave him the only ribbon that he had not yet received. That was the Order of St. George, which could only be gained by winning a battle in the field.

"Is it not evident that I am God's spoiled child?" he said gaily to de Ligne.

"Heaven protects you from yourself," answered de Ligne sharply. "Wear that ribbon out. You will soon have another."

The victory of Oczakov caused consternation in Europe. Catherine's suave charm had blinded European diplomats to her real aims. Suddenly they had a vision of a victorious Russian army swarming over the Middle East and appearing, as the Turks had done a hundred years before, at the very gates of Vienna. They decided quickly that the tottering Ottoman Empire must be propped up and that Russia should be diverted by a new war in the north.

Within a short time Catherine found herself in an almost desperate situation. Joseph II died, leaving her without an ally in the Turkish war. The French Revolution robbed her of the help of Louis XVI. England was angry because of Catherine's challenge to her in the American Revolutionary War.

The Russian Empress had not a friend left in Europe.

At this point Gustavus III, King of Sweden, declared war on Russia. He did this in the accepted eighteenth-century manner. At the beginning of the Turkish war, the handsome King had visited Catherine in St. Petersburg. He had sworn eternal peace and promised not to interfere in any war she cared to make. Returning home, he wrote her flattering letters. Then without warning he declared war. The war was short, and at its close Gustavus renewed his friendship.

"Let us forget our differences," he wrote, "like a storm that has passed."

Potemkin was furious that Catherine had let herself get involved in a war with Sweden, which he thought she could have prevented. He refused to release any of his troops from the Turkish campaign and called the new war an "old woman's war."

The "old woman's war," though neither long nor bloody, cost Russia 22 million rubles. Russia's finances were already disastrously low from the Turkish war. Catherine was forced to raise the taxes—putting an even greater burden on the unhappy serfs. She issued paper money in great quantities and Russia's financial balance was upset. Her country no longer had any credit in Europe.

Catherine realized finally that these wars were ruining Russia. "To make war three things are necessary," she wrote sadly to Potemkin, "money, money and money." Her dream of Alexander's empire was growing dim. She began to wish desperately for peace.

But peace was easier to wish for than to attain. After a vastly expensive series of entertainments in Moscow to celebrate the taking of Oczakov, Potemkin went south again, back to his ravaged army. The war dragged on hopelessly with small sorties and indecisive battles. The new Russian fleet, which had had a great success at Oczakov, now appeared to be impotent. Hoping to revive it Catherine sent for John Paul Jones, the courageous Scottish seaman who had won renown during the American Revolutionary War for his brilliant freelance operations against British ships. Jones was waiting restlessly in Paris for command of a new ship when Catherine's invitation came. The great adventurer accepted immediately and set out with a high heart to give the Russian navy new life. He was made an admiral and promised complete command. But he did not get it. British seamen had been in command of many of the Russian ships. Now they were angry and jealous that a rebel American was brought in over their heads. They sabotaged his work, sent in false reports and maligned his character to Catherine. He was given no credit for the small victories which the Russian navy began to make.

Catherine, unaware of the true facts, was disappointed in the famous sailor. She dismissed him, and he went sadly back to Paris. There he died in 1792, only forty-five years old, penniless and forgotten.

Catherine had a more personal worry during these unhappy war years. After Oczakov her despised and neglected son thrust himself into her consciousness again. He asked if he could serve in the Turkish war as a general. Catherine was afraid of what might happen if Paul became truly warlike. But she could not refuse outright. She gave him a half-promise. Then she took it back, using as an excuse the fact that his wife was about to have a baby. Paul confronted her, for once courageous in the presence of his feared and hated parent.

"What will be said of me," he demanded angrily, "if you make me abandon this project at the very moment of its execution? I shall be accused of cowardice at the approach of danger."

Catherine stared at him coldly. "It will be said that the Grand Duke is an obedient son," she replied. She began to study a paper on her desk and would say no more.

Paul stood before her in silence for several minutes, his face white and twitching with helpless rage. Then he left the room abruptly.

Later he asked for a military post in the Swedish war. Catherine could think of no excuse this time. She let him go. But he was given a subordinate position where he had no authority and nothing to do. A general was assigned to watch him constantly. When Paul saw that he had been frustrated again, he left the campaign in a fury and rushed back to St. Petersburg. But before he could complain to his mother, he fell desperately ill, ravaged and weakened by his violent anger. He recovered slowly and retired again to his country palace. There he was overtaken by a melancholy so deep that it was feared his sanity was gone forever.

In fact, he never entirely recovered from this final blow to his pride. From this time insanity gradually overtook him. Catherine had at last completed the ruin started by Elizabeth thirty-five years before.

Neither of the women who had cared for him so badly was entirely to blame. Paul was undoubtedly weak-minded to start with. His heritage was not good, and insanity ran in the family of Peter the Great. But possibly, if Elizabeth had not been so hysterical, and if his own mother had been tender instead of impatient, he would not have gone over the edge. Apparently, however, the dreadful curse died with Paul. Besides Alexander and Constantine, Paul had five other children. Alexandrina, born four years after Constantine, became a beautiful, open-hearted little girl. She, and the four that followed, their parents were allowed to keep. Marie, stolid, limited and kind, was a good mother. Her children were quite ordinary and sensible, apparently unaffected by the morose humors of their father. And in later years they never, not even the surly, withdrawn Constantine, developed the distressing symptoms of weakness and ferocity that had plagued the family of the czars for so many generations.

In 1790, after three years of war, the Russian army won its second important victory—the conquest of Ismael, a crucial port city on the delta of the Danube River. This bloody battle and the ruthless massacre that followed it were conducted not by Potemkin but by General Suvarov, a fearless and cruel military genius.

Now Catherine wrote to Potemkin that he must make peace at once. But the once brilliant diplomatist seemed as unable to make peace as he had been to make war. Again he lingered, alternately carousing and moping. This time it was not fear of battle that tortured him, but fear of his position. He had lost the confidence of his Queen. She sent her orders to others, and others won the battles.

With characteristic suddenness he left the south and hastened back to St. Petersburg. Before completing the Turkish war he would make an effort to regain Catherine's faith and devotion. He made a fatal mistake—he decided to rely on his charm instead of his brain. Always he had been able to charm her before. He would do so again. He would give a magnificent party, he would talk to her tenderly and gaily; and everything would be as it had been in the early years.

Catherine shivered with foreboding when she received the invitation to Potemkin's party. Just so had Gregory Orlov lingered instead of making peace; just so had he come rushing back to the capital; just so had he taken refuge in mindless entertainment. Was Potemkin too—the man she most loved and trusted —to go through the downward spiral of moodiness and madness? Sometimes, when she looked back on it, her life in Russia seemed to her like a round, with the sinister theme of self-destruction and insanity coming back again and again. What was the matter with these Russians, she asked herself again. She could not answer her own question, nor could anyone else. She had taken up her abode with the strangest people on earth.

Catherine had built for Potemkin a beautiful palace in St. Petersburg. He called it the Taurida Palace because it was a reward for the ancient southern kingdom he had won for her. On the night of Potemkin's final bid for his Queen's affection, the great Taurida Palace was lit from one end to the other with thousands of candles.

The outside of the palace was simple and classical, of white-plastered brick and tall slim columns. Inside it had all the expensive elegance that the eighteenth century could command. When Potemkin's guests began to arrive, they came out of the icy winter night into a scene that might have been southern Italy. The great main hall had neither furniture nor ornament except for a few tall, graceful vases of Carrara marble. All around the hall was a double row of fluted columns, and in the open center was a garden. Here tropical trees and flowers swayed in a gentle breeze, their delicate fragrance filling the hall. Bright-colored fish darted in tiny lakes and canals. In the middle of the garden was a statue of Catherine in Persian marble. Hidden lights spread a soft radiance over statue, leaves and blossoms, but the main light came from an immense crystal chandelier. Suspended from it was Catherine's monogram in paste diamonds, trembling and gleaming in the faintly moving air. The room was evenly warmed by hot water moving constantly through metal canals within the walls. In the soft,

scented air the visitors were almost surprised to look
out of the tall French windows on the ice and snow of
St. Petersburg's long winter.

Potemkin had invited every diplomat, every nobleman, every important official of the capital. Even
Catherine's son was there, dour and gloomy, his stout,
plain wife by his side. Three of the grandchildren
were there: Alexander, now fourteen but looking
younger; Constantine, glowering and awkward; Alexandrina, nine years old, a thin, shy, dainty child.

When the signal came that Catherine was arriving,
Potemkin ordered servants to distribute meat, clothing
and drinks to the crowds of curious people outside.
Thousands had gathered to watch the arrival of the
guests and peer through the windows at the lovely
tropical spectacle inside.

A spontaneous cheer went up as the aging but still
beautiful Empress descended from her carriage and
limped painfully through the entrance, supported on
each side by tall young courtiers. Catherine was now
sixty years old. Her youthful vigor had appeared in-
destructible as the years passed. Seemingly tireless, she
got through more work every day than her young
ministers and was still fresh for St. Petersburg's sparkling balls and receptions. But imperceptibly she was
growing older, stouter, slower. Her eyes were as merry
as ever as she surveyed the cheering crowd around
Prince Potemkin's palace. Her humor was as quick,
her mind as sharp as she spoke to the ladies and
gentlemen at the glittering reception. But when her
ready smile came, it could be seen that she had lost all
her teeth, just like any aging peasant woman. There
were no dentists in eighteenth-century Russia. Teeth

were just pulled out when they decayed, and it was an extraordinary person who still had any teeth left at sixty. Catherine's most painful sign of age was her heaviness. Though she ate frugally and drank not at all, she had grown immensely stout. Her small feet could hardly hold up her heavy body, and she was increasingly troubled with pains in her legs.

But she would not admit the coming of infirmity. She made fun of Frederick II, who had resigned himself to a wheel chair years before and sat in it all the time, grumpy and very sorry for himself. Although Catherine had to be supported on both sides, she insisted on walking—and she never missed a party.

As she entered the main hall, the orchestra of three hundred musicians played a stately hymn; and the whole gorgeous, bejeweled company bowed, rustling skirts sweeping the floor, diamond tiaras almost touching the ground. The Empress was conducted to a throne on a platform before the fragrant garden.

Forty-eight children, among them the three grandchildren, danced a formal ballet before her. They were all dressed in white and covered with jewels said to have cost ten million rubles. No one could accuse Potemkin of being stingy.

After this the entire company moved to another great hall with precious French medieval tapestries on its walls. In the center was an artificial elephant covered with rubies and emeralds. A Persian clad in many-colored garments of silk struck a gong, and a curtain rose on a large stage. The company watched a satirical comedy; then heard a men's chorus sing flowing, sorrowful Russian songs. There were national dances from many parts of the empire, and a procession representing all the peoples subject to Catherine's rule.

Through all this Potemkin stood beside Catherine's throne, often leaning over to speak to her. His one eye twinkled humorously, and Catherine's laugh rang out, young and happy. Always mistress of her emotions, Catherine had left at home her misgivings about this party and its purpose. She was ready to have a good time—and that was a talent that had come easily to her since girlhood.

When the entertainment was over, the whole palace was thrown open to the guests for supper and dancing. A table was laid for six hundred, while the rest wandered where they wished through the great rooms. The palace seemed on fire. Ten thousand candles burned; and their light was reflected dazzlingly from mirrors, sparkling stones, globes of glass.

Catherine, who usually retired at ten from even the most important parties, stayed on and on. The old Queen was really enjoying herself. She loved the flamboyant pageantry, of which only a Russian was capable. And among Russians only her Potemkin had such delightful imagination. She was enchanted, as always, by the rare charm of her difficult minister.

If only he would bring this dreadful, heart-breaking war to an end!

At midnight she finally called her courtiers to her. As she rose to leave, the orchestra once more played a hymn. She turned to her host to thank him. Overcome with emotion Potemkin sank to the floor before her. Then he raised himself to one knee, took her beautiful white hand in both of his, kissed it and wept over it. There were tears in Catherine's eyes as she turned away.

This was the most magnificent party that even glamorous St. Petersburg had ever seen. But Potemkin was dissatisfied. He could not tear himself away from the formal court life he had always so hated. Had he really won his Queen's devotion again? He must stay and find out. As he stayed, his soldiers were sickening and dying in the south; and the war was not yet over.

The astute Empress, though her heart as always leaned towards Potemkin, was not to be won by charm, wit, and extravagance. She sent orders to Prince Repnin, Potemkin's second in command in the south, to bring the war to a speedy close.

While Potemkin caroused and brooded in St. Petersburg, Repnin ordered an all-out offensive. Within two months the Turks were suing for peace. Repnin came to St. Petersburg to report to the Empress. She told him to start peace negotiations immediately.

Then Repnin went to see Potemkin. His commander in chief was in a rage and advanced on him threateningly.

"You little upstart, how dared you undertake so many things in my absence? Who gave you any such orders?" The single eye glowered angrily.

Repnin, equally hot-tempered, replied, "I have served my country, and my head is not at your disposal." He strode to the door, turned back and shouted, "You are a devil, whom I defy!" The door slammed behind him.

Potemkin followed him with clenched fist upraised. Now, too late, he saw his mistake. He had deserted the field of battle and left his work to others. He still burned with the old dream that he and his Queen had shared. If the dream was finished, he would die. He could not let Repnin take *his* victories. He could not allow Catherine to make peace and end forever the hope of a Byzantine Empire.

He would go back to the south and prolong the war at any cost.

But Potemkin was ill. His constant dissipations, alternating with the hard life of a soldier in the field, had undermined his health dangerously. Except for his imaginary headaches he had never paid any attention to physical ailments, and now he refused to admit the existence of a mortal illness. Dismissing his doctors contemptuously, he raced off to the south. He drove his horses without mercy and lived on salt meat, raw turnips and hot spiced wine.

On October 15, 1791, he had nearly reached Oczakov. Suddenly he started to suffocate. The coach stopped, and a servant spread his cloak by the roadside. Potemkin was carried out and laid on the ground. Above him was the soft blue southern sky, and around him the tall trees and flower-filled meadows of the lovely lands he had won for his mistress.

Within a few minutes he was dead.

When the news was brought to Catherine, she listened without a change of expression. But her face grew gray, and at the end of the report she fainted. As soon as she was brought around, she fainted again. When she finally came to, she stared wordlessly before her, oblivious of the anxious people hovering over her. For the first time in her life she felt old and abandoned.

One by one her friends and equals had died. And now Potemkin—her second self. What was there left for her? She felt that she was the last person in the eighteenth century.

10 The Last Autocrat

Alone and sad as she was, the old Queen had no intention of giving in to despair. As always she kept the reins of government firmly in her hands. At the beginning of 1792, three months after Potemkin had died, she signed the Treaty of Jassy with the Ottoman Empire. The Turks gave up forever all claims to the Crimea and Taurida. The lands of Moldavia and Wallachia adjoining Russia on the western shore of the Black Sea were made independent of the Sultan. A firm pledge was given that the Caucasian mountaineers would not attack the Russian border.

Now Russia controlled most of the Black Sea and could trade freely with all the countries of the Middle East. Her frontier extended in the south as far as the formidable Caucasus Mountains. There the shadow of Mt. Elbrus, the highest mountain in Europe, fell almost on the Russian border. For the first time Russian peasants tilling the fertile southern soil could feel secure, with the protective fortress of the giant mountain range behind them.

The sea outlet to the Mediterranean and the dream of a new Byzantine Empire were still unrealized hopes. They would never be realized. Catherine, growing older, had also grown more realistic. She knew now that Europe would never allow Russia to expand beyond its natural boundaries. Catherine had helped to establish those natural boundaries, and she was almost content.

An event that disturbed her far more deeply than the failure of the Byzantine project was the French Revolution, which had started in 1789. Oddly, the self-satisfied monarchs of the eighteenth century, highly educated and liberal as they were, had not really believed that peasants would ever rise against their masters. The American Revolution had seemed far away and heroic. Besides, the American colonists were not peasants like this atrocious rabble that was committing such bloody excesses in France.

In spite of Catherine's deep-rooted liberalism, revolutionary France seemed to her rough and anarchic. It was quite unlike the ideal state envisaged by her revered Voltaire. Still fresh in her mind was the dreadful, disorganized rebellion led by the adventurer

Pugachev. Deeper than that was her sense of guilt at the misery of Russia's millions of slave serfs, whom she had been unable to help.

She showed her fear by appearing shocked and angry. "A cordon ought to be drawn around France," she said sternly to the Prince de Ligne, "as is done against the plague."

"Your Majesty is right," answered the suave courtier. "Liberty is truly an excellent thing, but it is going into bad hands. Rascals appoint themselves ministers to a captive king, and young men who cannot pay their tailors' bills want to pay the debts of the state. Let us stop this quickly and strenuously."

But Catherine did not want to fight France. Although she feared and hated the raw new democracy, she now feared and hated war even more. She contented herself with bluster and threats. Unreasonably angry at the dead Voltaire, she had his bust taken out of her study and thrown into the dust bin. She called George Washington a rebel and reviled the Americans, whom she had so much admired for their courage a few years before. She spoke a great deal of marching against France. But she tried to arrange that Prussia, Austria and England should do the fighting.

Her bluster was made fun of, and her threats were not taken seriously. Everyone knew that the wily old lady would handle things as she liked behind the scenes, whatever she said in public.

But foreigners who visited Russia were astounded at the freedom they found there. Frightened and angry as Catherine was, she would not let go her principles of tolerance and free speech. As long as she felt her country was safe, she let men talk as they pleased.

Russia, the country of slavery, was intellectually the freest land in all Europe in those fearful, fanatical years at the end of the century. In Italy anyone who sang French revolutionary songs was imprisoned. In Vienna French was not allowed to be spoken. All over Europe Frenchmen were being thrown into jail and massacred.

But their compatriots, whether republican or royalist, aired their opinions in the court of the Empress of Russia, and walked the streets of St. Petersburg without fear. A fiery Swiss Republican, a man openly sympathetic to the French Revolution, was the chief tutor to the Grand Dukes Alexander and Constantine. The young royal Dukes chanted French revolutionary songs in the palaces of the czars and carried French revolutionary cockades in their pockets. In St. Petersburg lived, unmolested, the brother of Marat, one of the most violent of the French revolutionists. After the death of Louis XVI under the guillotine, all Frenchmen in Russia, whatever their politics, were placed under the protection of the Russian crown. This was to save them—not from persecution by Russian citizens—but from the anger of foreigners living in Russia.

The air of intellectual freedom blew fresh over Russia in Catherine's day as it had never before, nor has since.

By 1796 Catherine, now sixty-seven years old, could look back clear-eyed on her fifty-two years in Russia and feel pride. She had suffered some sorrows and some defeats; for some things done wrong she felt remorse. But she had been a good queen. Although her century was coming to an end, Catherine still stood stanch, a monument to a graceful way of life that existed no more.

She called to her Leo Narishkin—the same dashing courtier who had met the shy fourteen-year-old at the border of Russia; who had played blindman's buff, stood on his head and meowed like a cat to make her laugh during the dismal years of her marriage. Narishkin was now a sad, fat old man. But he was the only one left who still remembered her gay days and her proud days.

Catherine sat in her study. She wore her favorite blue velvet tunic, with a full-sleeved, high-necked Russian blouse of fine thin cotton, delicately embroidered. Her cheeks were rouged and her fine, heavy hair was thickly streaked with gray. But her voice was firm and her eyes as bright as ever.

"When I traveled from Stettin," she said, "we were so poor that I had to borrow a dress from the sister of Frederick of Prussia to go to dinner."

"I remember you in your plain traveling dress at Riga," said Narishkin. "How your eyes sparkled when you saw the sable capes. I think you had never owned a fur before."

"No, I had not," said the Empress, looking with satisfaction at the huge diamond solitaire on her third finger. "I reached Russia penniless. But I shall not die in debt to the Empire, for I leave her the Crimea and Poland as my portion."

She turned thoughtful. "But there is still one thing to do," she said. "Our boundaries are safe everywhere except in the north. I do not trust the new King of Sweden. His father has made trouble for us before. The son can do so again. There must be an alliance which will last."

"Alexandrina!" whispered Narishkin. The Queen smiled. The same thought had been in her mind.

Later that day she wrote a letter to the young King of Sweden. The son of her good friend, Gustavus III, must visit her in St. Petersburg. How happy a time she had had with his father when he visited her, and how charming were the letters of Sweden's new King. When he came she would like him to pay especial attention to her lovely granddaughter, Alexandrina, now fourteen, of an age to be betrothed.

Gustavus IV responded immediately with enthusiasm. An alliance with Russia would be a windfall for his small, poor country.

The whole court assembled to greet the Swedish King on his arrival. At the entrance of the great reception hall, he waited for Catherine. When she appeared, he sank on one knee and took her hand to kiss it. But she raised it immediately.

"I cannot forget that the son of my friend is now a king," she said, smiling. "It is not meet for my hand to be kissed by a king."

Gustavus answered, "If your Majesty will not give me permission as an empress, at least allow me as a lady, to whom I owe so much respect and admiration."

He then kissed her hand and held it in his as they entered the hall together. The court caught its breath as the two entered hand in hand. Catherine, in a white satin court dress, sparkling with jewels, her hair dressed high, her figure straight as a girl's in spite of her stoutness, looked like a goddess. Beside her the tall young King, only seventeen years old, his golden hair reaching nearly to his shoulders, appeared a chivalrous knight.

They went straight to Alexandrina. As she had been taught, the young Princess curtsied to the ground, her head bowed. Then she looked shyly up at the noble young man who was to be her husband. She was utterly unable to say a word. Alexandrina was tall for her age and very slender; and her skin was pale as alabaster. Flaxen hair fell in soft natural ringlets on each side of her lovely, sensitive face. Every line of her expressed innocence and delicacy.

There were tears in Catherine's eyes as she looked at the two silent and embarrassed youngsters. Nearly fifty years ago she had had that candid innocence. She had come, filled with hope, to meet her witless bridegroom.

Alexandrina shall be happy, she thought fiercely.

During the days that followed Catherine saw to it that Gustavus and Alexandrina were together constantly. She watched them anxiously for signs of affection. She watched them as they sat together at supper, exchanging a few shy words. She watched them as they played word games or drew pictures in her little drawing room in the evenings, Alexandrina's face lighting with a rare smile. She watched her grandchild blush delicately one evening when Gustavus took her hand with tenderness, watched as he kissed her at the door when the evening was over. The old Empress was sentimental over this slowly blooming love. It seemed herself that she was watching—a new and happier and luckier Catherine.

St. Petersburg was festive in honor of the charming visitor. Catherine, who had not gone out much since the death of Potemkin, gained new vigor and gaiety. She did not miss a ball, and she radiated happiness.

Only one thing marred her joy. That was the behavior of Constantine, her second grandson. He acted like a vulgar boor, embarrassing his grandmother by his contrast with the perfect manners of the enchanting Swedish King. Once, while Gustavus watched an army review, Constantine was seen running and yelling behind the lines of soldiers. He imitated them grotesquely and started to beat some of them. Catherine was so incensed at this display that she ordered Constantine to be confined to his room during all public ceremonies.

She felt an uneasy distress at the behavior of this carefully nurtured grandson. Deeply jealous of his attractive and talented older brother, Constantine had at an early age refused to study, calling his tutor an addlepated nincompoop. When he had become engaged, he had showed his affection to his fiancée by banging a drum and blowing a trumpet in her breakfast room in the mornings. At other times he twisted her arm and bit her. He engaged in gun practice with rats, which he loaded alive into the cannons as ammunition.

To Catherine it was like a horrible repeating nightmare. Forty years earlier her husband had tortured her senses with a violin, shouted at her, beat his dogs and hung dead rats upon gallows. Was there to be no end to the chain of insanity in this cursed family?

But Catherine had always expected too much of the dull-witted Constantine. He was not crazy. His jealousy of his elder brother made him do everything wrong, almost in protest. He would never be king of Greece—nor king of anything at all. But he would live to be a normal, if somewhat sulky and silent, man.

Catherine could not see into the future. But she determinedly shook off her fear as the round of gaiety continued and the beautiful youngsters became daily more tender with each other. One of the balls was given at a nobleman's house on the Neva River. Just as Catherine's carriage drove up to the door a flaming meteor shot out of the sky and sank into the Neva with a fearful hiss, clouds of steam rising above it. There was a sudden horrified silence in the group around the Empress. Then a voice whispered, "Evil omen."

Catherine was shocked in spite of herself. But when she heard the whisper, she turned sharply to the speaker. "Nonsense!" she said in a brisk tone. Her face had its accustomed pleasant friendliness as she entered the gate.

But she resolved to delay no longer. The next morning she would see Gustavus and arrange a treaty and marriage contract.

Her session with the Swedish King lasted a long time. He was young, but he was astute; and his advisers had warned him to beware of the cunning old diplomatist. Catherine wanted to put into the treaty a clause obligating Sweden to act against revolutionary France. She also insisted that her granddaughter be allowed to keep her religion. Remembering the terrible weeks of struggle with her conscience when she had forced herself to break with her own religion, she wanted to spare Alexandrina.

But Gustavus was king of a country which had always been the stanchest champion of the Protestant faith. He felt that his wife must be of his country's religion. Also he, no more than Catherine, wished his country to become involved in a European war. He would not sign anything, but took the papers to his ministers.

Weeks dragged on. The balls continued, but Catherine began to look pale and worried. She tired easily, and her friendly smile came less often. There was an uneasy atmosphere in the extravagant frivolity. At one of the last balls everyone came in heavy black mourning, for the death of the Queen of Portugal three and a half thousand miles away. When Catherine entered, also in mourning, she looked around the room and shook her head sadly.

"This ball looks more like a German funeral than a joyous entertainment," she said. She was unrouged, and her face was white with strain. The young Swedish King was also pale, and he hardly spoke to Alexandrina that night.

Finally he sent word to Catherine that he would sign an amended treaty. Catherine rejoiced once more. She ordered the whole court to assemble in full dress for the betrothal ceremony. The nobility gathered at seven o'clock in the throne room. There were long-bearded bishops in richly embroidered robes, covered with jewels; courtiers in velvet breeches of startling colors; princesses and countesses with wide satin, pearl-encrusted skirts. All the pomp and glory of Russia were there in rich display.

Alexandrina, her pale cheeks faintly pink-tinged with excitement, was dressed like a bride, in white silk. Catherine sat on her golden throne with a purple mantle over her shoulders and a diamond crown on her head. Everyone stood, silent and formal, awaiting the arrival of the royal bridegroom.

An hour passed, but Gustavus did not come. Another hour and another went by. The satin skirts rustled; the courtiers fidgeted. Conversation whispered through the hall:

"What is the matter? Has the King taken ill?"

"He is not very gallant. How dare he make the sovereign wait in the apartment of her very throne?"

At ten in the evening a messenger approached Catherine and whispered something to her. She rose convulsively, tried to speak, fell back again, almost fainting. Her courtiers sprang to her side and helped her out of the throne. There was shocked silence as she limped painfully through the great hall, through the lines of gaudy elegance. She looked straight before her, and her face was gray beneath the rouge.

When she had left, uneasy mutters ran through the crowd like wind before a storm. A herald appeared on the throne platform and announced in a loud, formal tone that the King of Sweden was ill and the ceremony would be postponed. The courtiers turned to one another, and the mutters grew angry and loud as their expressions changed from surprise to anger. The court disintegrated into little groups. Slowly, in disorganized fashion, they drifted out of the throne room.

The articles of marriage had been brought to Gustavus at six o'clock the evening of the betrothal. He read them. When he had finished, he stood up and threw the papers on the table.

"I will not sign," he said. "I cannot sign." The young King paced up and down the room, angry and distressed. "Sweden will not be a slave to Russia. The Empress cannot tell me what my country must do. I will not sign."

At the last minute Catherine had inserted the very terms that the Swedish King had refused earlier. She had made them gentler and changed the wording in a subtle way so that the King might not notice. But she had underestimated this young man, wise for all his seventeen years, and fiercely proud of the independence of his country.

His ministers wanted him to accept. They walked back and forth with him, pleading and arguing. The Russian Empress did not ask too much, they said. But Gustavus would not listen. He ordered them out of his room and locked the door. Until ten o'clock he remained alone, while his conscience fought with his love. Then he opened the door and called a messenger.

"Tell the Empress there will be no marriage," he said.

No one knew what had happened. They could only see that their Queen had been humiliated. For days speculation ran wild. Catherine refused to see anyone. But Gustavus continued to appear at court functions, now silent and stern. Alexandrina wilted visibly as the King ignored her. The frail child seemed to turn old and haggard before the eyes of the court.

The final romantic dream of Catherine's old age was shattered. Also, somehow, her diplomacy had failed. The double defeat was a fearful shock to her, and for several days she was ill. But she refused to let herself be bedridden. As soon as possible she began appearing at the balls and receptions again. But all the life had gone out of them. The court sighed with relief when Gustavus' visit came to an end.

Now Catherine seemed to have lost the heart for gaiety. She kept to her room and always supped alone. Even the grandchildren were allowed to visit her only once or twice a week. She felt old and ill and unhappy.

She revived briefly one morning a few weeks after Gustavus had left. News came to her that the Austrian Army had defeated the French in an important battle. She smiled—the dangerous new rabble had not won yet. There was still courage left in the soldiers of the old regime. She wrote a note to the Austrian ambassador in her old gay vein:

"I hasten to inform your excellent excellency that the excellent troops of your excellent court have given the French an excellent drubbing."

She felt good the whole day. The next morning, as she settled briskly down to business at her desk, she looked brighter and happier than she had at any time since the humiliation of Alexandrina. For an hour her secretaries and messengers were kept busy. Then she asked to be excused for a few minutes and went into her bedroom. The secretary who was waiting at her desk heard nothing for a long time.

Suddenly there was a scream from her room. He rushed in. Catherine lay on the floor, unconscious, her face dark red. Quickly he called her servants. Afraid to move her, they took the mattress from her bed, laid it on the floor and gently lifted the Empress onto it.

She had had a stroke, but she was not dead. For two days she lay on the floor, her body alive but her voice mute. Candles were lighted in the dim, curtained room, and two ladies-in-waiting sat always beside her, weeping quietly.

When Paul heard that his mother was dying, he rushed to the palace. Briefly and coldly he surveyed the helpless Empress. Then he installed himself in a little office just beyond his mother's bedroom. As if already emperor, he feverishly gave orders and sent messengers. The messengers had to go through the sickroom, stepping over Catherine's body.

The ladies-in-waiting watched this unnatural bustle fearfully as they sat despairing beside their unconscious Queen. Everyone was afraid of the horrors to come if Catherine should die and her ferocious son become emperor.

But Catherine's son was more frightened than anyone. How long would his mother last? Would she ever be able to speak again and deprive him of the throne? He had searched frantically through her papers seeking for evidence that she had disowned him and made Alexander her heir. He had found nothing—but still she might speak.

Happily for Paul the power of speech was gone forever. On November 10, 1796, at eleven in the evening, Catherine died, still silent.

"All is at an end!" cried one of her ladies, "she and our happiness."

In truth all was at an end. Russia had seen the days of her greatest glory and the last of her great monarchs. Catherine and her century had ended together. The witty, cultured, gracious Empress had been a perfect expression of her age: the age of reason, of philosophy, of courtly elegance, of polished wit—and of uncompromising autocracy. At the end she had stood alone, proud and sad, the winds of freedom blowing around her.

A new age was dawning, frightening and stormy. Catherine had lived only to see its beginnings, in bloody anarchy. She and her brilliant contemporaries had never known its promise—the promise of equality for all men.

But the gay German Princess with freedom in her heart had herself helped to shape the democracy which was to destroy all her kind. She had brought to Russia its first breath of equality and justice—and for this she is more to be remembered than for all the glorious pageantry of her long reign.

Index

Alexander (Catherine's grandson), 132, 141-42, 145, 157, 160, 169, 179

Alexandrina (Catherine's granddaughter), 157, 160, 171-72, 174-75, 178

American Revolution, 124, 136-37, 154-55, 167

Azov, province of, 113, 118

August, Prince Christian, 4-5
See also Fike, father of

Austria, 123, 148

Black Sea, 113, 119, 127, 151, 166-67

Boyars, 88-90

Bruemmer, 16

Brunswick, court of, 13, 14

Byzantium, 128-29, 132, 147, 167

Cardel, Babet, 5-8, 10, 21

Card-playing, by Russian nobility, 27, 39, 59

Catherine, Grand Duchess, ballet lessons of, 43
  in collapse of house, 58-59
  debts of, 68
  and Elizabeth, Empress, unfriendliness of, 51-53
  father of, death of, 53
  and Frederick II, 66
  friends at court, 64-65
  future of Russia planned by, 64
  generosity of, 67
  maids-in-waiting of, 44-45
  at masquerade ball, 44
  in Moscow, 60, 62
  mother of, 42-43, 47, 52-54
  and Peter, betrothal to, 42
    marriage to, 50ff., 65ff.
    misgivings prior to, 47
    plays with, 43
    talks with, before marriage, 46
  plays written by, 66
  reading by, 54-55
  reproved for frivolity, 45-46
  son of, 65

wedding of, 47-49
See also Catherine the Great; Fike

Catherine the Great, 87, 89-90
  and American Revolution, 124, 136-37, 154-55, 167
  appearance of, 85
  beauty of, 85
  as benevolent despot, 66-107 passim
  Byzantium as goal of, 128-29, 132, 147, 167
  cat owned by, 141
  as conqueror, 109, 111, 127
  correspondence of, 133-34
  court of, 140, 145-46
  Crimea annexed by, 119
  on Crimean tour, 121-28
  death of, 179
  at fifty, 131
  fleet begun by, 128
  and French Revolution, 154, 167ff.
  granddaughter of, 157, 160, 171-172, 174-75, 178
  grandsons of, 132, 140-44, 160, 169, 173, 179
  grasp of character by, 86
  and Gustavus IV, 171-78
  intelligence of, 86, 145
  law reforms of, 102-04
  and Orlov brothers, 73-74, 76-77, 98-101, 112-14, 158
  and Peter, death of, 84
    insult by, 72
    revolution against, 74-80
  plays written by, 131-32
  plot against, by Ivan's supporters, 94-95
  and Poland, partition of, 110-11, 126-27
  and Potemkin, Gregory, see Potemkin, Gregory
  reforms of, 95-96, 102-04, 106-07, 134
  religious observances of, 135
  Senate instructed in geography, 95
  at sixty, 160

Catherine the Great (*cont.*)
  at sixty-seven, 169
  son of, 80-81, 97-98, 132, 137-38,
    143, 156-57, 179
  and Sweden, war with, 154, 156
  at thirty-three, 85
  and Turks, treaties with, 113, 166
    wars with, 101, 112, 148*ff.*
  uprising against, by Cossacks, 104,
    106
  vaccination sponsored by, 100-
    101
  See also Catherine, Grand Duch-
    ess; Fike
Cherson, 127-28
"Chlore, Journey of," 133
Constantine (Catherine's grandson), 132, 141-42, 157, 169,
  173
Constantinople, 124, 128-29, 132,
  148
Cossacks, 104, 106, 118, 150
Crimea, 119, 121, 148, 166, 170
Cronstadt, 78

Dashkov, Princess, 72-73
Democracy, road to, 86-87
Denmark, 71, 74
Diderot, 134

Elephants, in St. Petersburg, 25, 28
Elizabeth, Empress, of Russia, 18,
    22-23, 25, 28, 35, 37, 39, 157
  appearance of, 36
  Catherine scolded by, 51
  and Catherine's son, 65
  at Catherine's wedding, 48
  costumes of, 36
  court frequently transferred by,
    43, 58
  death of, 68
  Fike bled on orders of, 38-39
  Fike introduced to, 36
  funeral of, 69-70
  gifts to Fike, 40, 42
  Ivan imprisoned by, 94
  masquerade balls given by, 44
  Peter adopted by, 17-18
  Peter banished from dinner table,
    56
  plot against, 67
  self-indulgence of, 38
  tyranny of, 52

Feodor, Prince, 84
Feudal system, 89

Fike, accident to, 12
  and Babet, 5-8, 10, 21
  birth of, 5
  brothers of, 10-11
  at Brunswick, 13-14
  education of, 5, 7-9
  and Elizabeth, Empress, 36, 40
  father of, 11-12, 19-20, 22, 30-31.
    See also August, Prince
    Christian.
  and Frederick I, 13
  and Frederick II, 21-22
  generosity of, 40
  gifts from Empress Elizabeth, 40
  and Greek Orthodox Church, 37,
    40-42
  and Henry, Prince, of Prussia, 14
  and Moscow, arrival in, 31-34
    court in, 35-38
    illness in, 38-39
  mother of, 5, 10-13, 17-23, 33, 35-
    39, 42
  and Peter, as childhood friends,
    17
    meeting with, 15
    planning of marriage to, 18*ff.*
  and Russia, arrival in, 23-24
    three resolutions on, 31-32
    village huts of, 28-30
  Russian learned by, 37, 40
  and St. Petersburg, arrival in, 25
    delicacies in, 25
    elephants displayed in, 25, 28
    ice slide enjoyed in, 26-28
    new hairdo tried in, 27-28
    sleigh race watched in, 26
  self-discipline of, 38
  tone-deafness of, 8
  and Wagner, Pastor, 7-8, 37, 45,
    58
  See also Catherine, Grand Duch-
    ess; Catherine the Great
Frederick I, of Prussia, 4, 13
Frederick II, of Prussia, 18, 21-22,
    57, 66, 70-71, 97, 109-10, 133,
    138, 161
French Revolution, 154, 167*ff.*

Gambling, by Russian nobility, 27,
    62
George, Prince, of Holstein, 71
George III, of England, 136
Greece, 124, 142
Greek Orthodox Church, 37, 40-41,
    67
Grimm, Friedrich Melchior, 133
Gustavus III, of Sweden, 154, 171
Gustavus IV, of Sweden, 171-78

Henry, Prince, of Prussia, 14
Hessen-Homburg, Prince of, 35
Holstein, duchy of, 56, 66, 71, 83

Ice slide, Fike's enjoyment of, 26-27
Ikon worship, 30, 63
Ismael, 157
Ivan, Prince, 94-95
Izbiten, 29

Jassy, Treaty of, 166
Johanna, Princess, 5, 10-13, 17-23,
    33, 35-39, 42-43, 52-53
Jones, John Paul, 155
Joseph II, of Austria, 106, 123-24,
    126, 128, 133, 148, 151, 154

Kiev, 125
Kvass, 91

Ligne, de, Prince, 133, 151-53, 168
Louis XVI, of France, 139, 154, 169

Maria Theresa, Empress, of Austria,
    109-10, 123, 127
Marie, Princess, 98, 137-38, 143, 157
Mediterranean Sea, 128-29, 167
Moldavia, 151, 166
Mon Plaisir, 74, 77
Moscow, 92, 94, 111, 114, 121, 127
    Archbishop of, and smallpox, 101
    bell of, 34-35
    Fike's arrival in, 31-34
    smallpox in, 100-01
    unkemptness of, 60

Narishkin, Leo, 23, 25-27, 34, 71,
    115, 124, 170-71
Neva River, 26, 70, 174

Oczakov, 151-56, 164
Orlov, Alexei, 74-75, 79, 83-84
Orlov, Gregory, 76-77, 99, 101, 112-
    114, 158
Ottoman Empire, 109, 111ff., 147,
    149
    and Russia, treaties with, 113-14,
    166
    wars with, 101, 112, 148-56, 158,
    163

Paul (Catherine's son), 65, 80-81,
    97-98, 132, 137-39, 143, 156-
    157, 179
Peasants, Russian, 28-31
    Catherine's plans for, 86, 90, 94
    cleanliness of, 92
    religion of, 88
    shrewdness of, 93
Peter (Catherine's husband), 15, 17,
    35-37, 39, 43
    Catherine feared by, 67, 71
    Catherine insulted by, 72
    death of, 84
    dogs trained by, 57, 61
    as Emperor, 68-74
        abdication of, 78-80
    Frederick II admired by, 57
    and Holstein, 56, 66
    Lutheran services for, 67
    mental derangement of, 55-57
    in plot against Elizabeth, 67
    punished by Bruemmer, 16
    at Ropsha, 82-83
    smallpox contracted by, 47
    violin played by, 57, 61
    weakness of, 16, 46
    See also Catherine, Grand Duch-
        ess, and Peter; Catherine the
        Great, and Peter; Fike, and
        Peter
Peter the Great, 18, 25, 81, 88-89,
    107, 157
Poland, 109, 126-27, 170
    partition of, 110-11
Poniatovsky, 110, 126-27
Potemkin, Gregory, 99, 101, 122-
    123, 129, 147
    as Azov governor, 118-19
    beating of, by Orlovs, 100
    and Catherine, 115
        correspondence with, 134
        Crimea displayed to, 126-28
        love for, 73, 99, 114, 116
        plume offered to, 76-77, 99
        at Taurida Palace, 159ff.
    death of, 164-66
    as monk, 114-15
    parties given by, 120-21, 159ff.
    personality of, 116-17, 120
    as Prince of Taurida, 119, 128
    and Repnin, 163-64
    as statesman, 113-14
    and Turks, treaty negotiated
        with, 113-14
    in wars with, 100, 112, 148, 150-
    155, 158
    wealth of, 117

Priests, Russian, 62-63
Pugachev, 106, 168

Repnin, Prince, 163-64
Riga, 23
Ropsha, 82-83
Russia, in eighteenth century, 4-5
  army of, 148-49
  communications in, poor, 94
  drunkenness in, 93
  fertility of soil of, 91
  Fike's arrival in, 23-24
  food in, abundance of, 91-92
  freedom in, after French Revolu-
    tion, 168-69
  friendliness in, 91, 93
  future of, planned by Grand
    Duchess Catherine, 86, 90, 94
  language of, 90
  law in, 102*ff.*
  longevity of people of, 91
  map of, 105
  as musical nation, 90-91
  slavery in, 26, 62, 87, 90, 94, 104,
    106-07
  superstitions in, 62-63, 94
  theft in, 93
  village huts of, 28-30, 92
  in war with Sweden, 154, 156
  in wars with Turks, 101, 112, 148-
    156, 158, 163
  women in, 87

St. Petersburg, 23-26, 60, 74, 92-94,
    113, 156, 158, 163
  built with slave labor, 26
  Catherine's flight to, 74-75
  English merchants in, 136
  Fike's arrival in, 25
  French revolutionists in, 169
  Gustavus IV in, 171*ff.*
  poor housing in, 60
  rebuilt by Catherine, 96
  Summer Palace in, 59
  Taurida Palace in, 159*ff.*
Slavery, in Russia, 26, 62, 87, 90,
    94, 104, 106-07
Stettin, 4-5, 12, 170
Suvarov, General, 158
Sweden, 154, 156, 170

Tartars, 109, 111, 113, 118-20, 123
Taurida, 119, 166
Taurida Palace, 159*ff.*
Todorsky, Simon, 39-40
Tsarskoe Selo, 130, 133, 148

Voltaire, 55, 65, 86, 133-34, 136,
    167-68

Wagner, Pastor, 7-8, 37, 45, 58
Wallachia, 151, 166
Washington, George, 124, 168